CHAMPIONS OF FAITH

CHAMPIONS OF FAITH

Catholic Sports Heroes Tell Their Stories

Thomas O'Toole

Foreword by
Allyson Treloar

A SHEED & WARD BOOK

ROWMAN & LITTLEFIELD PUBLISHERS, INC.
Lanham • Boulder • New York • Toronto • Oxford

A SHEED & WARD BOOK

ROWMAN & LITTLEFIELD PUBLISHERS, INC.

Published in the United States of America
by Rowman & Littlefield Publishers, Inc.
A wholly owned subsidary of The Rowman & Littlefield Publishing Group, Inc.
4501 Forbes Boulevard, Suite 200, Lanham, Maryland 20706
www.rowmanlittlefield.com

PO Box 317
Oxford
OX2 9RU, UK

Printed in the United States of America

Cover design: Kathy Kikkert
Interior design: GrafixStudio, Inc.
Author photo by Jeanette O'Toole
Additional photo credits, page 231

Library of Congress Cataloging-in-Publication Data

O'Toole, Thomas (Thomas Augustine)
    Champions of faith : Catholic sports heroes tell their stories /
  Thomas O'Toole ;
    foreword by Allyson Treloar.
      p. cm.
    ISBN 1-58051-091-4
    1. Catholic athletes—United States—Interviews.
    2. Catholic coaches (Athletics)—United States—Interviews.
    3. Christian life—Catholic authors. I. Title.
BX4669 .O86 2001
282' .092'273—dc21
  [B]   00-06952

Contents

Dedication

To my mom and dad,
whose earthly prayers and sufferings
sustained me through this volume.

And to my friend, Sam,
who, although he died at book's beginning,
no doubt interceded in purgatory and heaven until its
completion.

And lastly, to my wife, Jeanette,
who not only put her blood, sweat,
and prayers into the project,
but *lived* with me throughout—
certainly the most saintly feat of all.

"Lord Jesus, have mercy on me, a sinner."

"O Mary, conceived without sin,
pray for us who have recourse to thee."

(The author's two constant prayers)

Acknowledgments

To Jeremy Langford, editor-in-chief of Sheed & Ward, who patiently endured all my frantic phone messages, scary e-mails, and missed deadlines.

And Anthony Chiffolo, my "agent" who not only got the ball rolling, but picked up the fumble when our first team dropped it.

I could not have written about these champions of faith in God if not for your faith in me.

Foreword

In my experience, there is a sense of community that is created when playing athletics in a Catholic environment. The community is bonded by the belief in God and in the desire to be successful in the athletic arena. Following Christ is shown out on the floor in game situations. How many times has a player looked up to thank God for victory? Or what about the prayers that are said before games? I played on a Catholic high school team, where the last part of a pre-game speech consisted of the entire team gathered together with hands joined in the center, heads bowed, speaking the Hail Mary, and then asking for Mary, Queen of Victory, to pray for us. That's when we broke apart and headed up the stairs to the gym. You just would not get that in a public school.

In my opinion, the greatest example of this type of program was held under Lou Holtz while at the University of Notre Dame. He created a program that inspired individuals to come to the university not only to play football, but to learn lessons—not just lessons within the classroom walls, but those lessons that equip young individuals for the rest of their lives in the real world. Holtz required that players make a commitment to themselves and to their teammates, to play with heart and to play for one another, not for the glory of the media. Lou Holtz is a man that models Christ to the best of his ability, and it truly shows in the eyes of the players past, as well as those he touched outside of football. This sense of community has since been brought to the University of South Carolina. They are definitely lucky to have such a wonderful person involved in developing a program.

I was fortunate to have learned from Lou as well. As my peers held interests in Michael Jackson and Alex P. Keaton from the TV sitcom "Family Ties" in the third grade, I was looking up to Lou Holtz. At age nine, I wrote to Lou after a University of Southern California win, and it turned into a ten-year correspondence. What an impact that has on a person at such a young age! He heard about my stories of volleyball and basketball, or my questions about the Desert Storm War, even about the colleges I applied to—Notre Dame, of course, being an option! Lou taught me about remaining positive after a loss, and showed me about the traditions that go along with being a part of the Notre Dame community. Who else would have taken the time to make a stranger feel so special?

Lou Holtz is the example I use, as he is the sports hero I got to know and love. Tom O'Toole has taken the time to get to know and write about fourteen of the greatest athletes and Catholic coaches of various sports. This is an opportunity for them to share their stories with individuals everywhere. Read their stories and learn. They are truly a testament to how our lives should be led in the glory of Christ.

Enjoy this book. Share it with your family and friends.

God Bless, and *Go Irish!*
Allyson Treloar
(Lou Holtz's #1 Fan)

Introduction

In the following pages, you will find fourteen varied accounts of—and encounters with—Catholic sports heroes. While a great number of you have no doubt already read of their athletic exploits in sports pages past and present, few fans have been privileged to hear about the spiritual strength that existed behind their triumphs. My documenting these *champions of faith* is an attempt to change that fact.

It is interesting to note that, while St. Paul often used sports as a metaphor for the soul's struggle with good and evil, and our evangelical Protestant brothers and sisters are often quick to mention Jesus as the force behind their athletic success, Catholics have been reluctant to credit Christ when the mikes are on and the cameras are rolling. Sports are a very sacramental part of life, and thus the reception of the sacraments would seem essential for the participant to put the contest into proper perspective. Perhaps therein lies the source of the dilemma: although Catholic athletes do see—and readily accept—the reality that sports figures are role models, their humility also reminds them of the far greater truth, that they are not yet saints.

I believe it is in this light that these champions would hope to be seen, as imperfect heroes still striving for the heroic virtue that will make them champions on the next level (that is, heaven) as well.

As far as the individual stories go, the length of one chapter versus another is due to my longer personal involvement with the story or subject, and has nothing to do with the individual's faith or character. Similarly, the fact that the book features more coaches than athletes, more football and basketball stars than those of other sports, and more men than women is not a reflection of my choice, because for each person who accepted the call, a dozen others rejected it. And just as with the story of the Great Feast (see Luke 14:15–24), we went with those who showed up.

What I did choose was to pursue this volume to the finish, despite great cost in time, money, and reputation (quitting a higher paying position to pursue these elusive champions despite the fact I have a wife and four kids to support), greater than anyone could have imagined. However, now that it is complete, I look at the book as my pearl of great price (see Matthew 14:44–46), and the wisdom and friendships I have gained in its writing as worth far more than I gave up. If readers gain a mere fraction of the faith I did in getting to know these fine men and women, the reading will be well worth their effort.

1. Sacred Elbows

The Forward Faith of Father John Smyth

An argument arose among the disciples about which of them was the greatest. Jesus realized the intention of their hearts and took a child and placed it by his side and said "Whoever receives this child in my name receives me, and whoever receives me receives the one who sent me. For the one who is least among all of you is the one who is the greatest."

—Luke 9:46-48

The main lobby in Maryville Academy, located in Des Plaines, Illinois, contains a trophy case whose contents are unlike any in this world. Besides memorabilia donated by the likes of fellow "champions of faith" Lou Holtz, Ray Meyer, and Mike Ditka, and such prominent Protestant brothers as Michael Jordan, Scottie Pippen, and Walter Payton, there are treasures from rock stars such as Pete Townshend and plaques denoting lavish contributions from huge corporations such as Coca-Cola. And, while all the arranged awards have been given in honor of one man—John Smyth, former Fightin' Irish basketball forward and enforcer, and current priest and Maryville director—he is the first to tell you that none of these gifts are his. One and all, these mighty trinkets belong to his kids, who, one and all, are his true treasures. Gazing into the trophy case, you realize the truth of former Notre Dame teammate and current Los Angeles Dodger executive Tommy Hawkins' statement, "I don't care what you do or what your occupation is, you cannot meet Father John without being affected by him." But it is in meeting him *and* seeing what he does with the kids that make almost everyone he comes into contact with want to give something *back*.

The scope of Maryville (and its sister campuses) is difficult to describe, and the manner in which one man holds it all together can only be viewed as miraculous. More than sixteen thousand youths were cared for in some way in 1999 by Maryville, whose members include everyone from full-time residents rescued from abusive homes, to college students who graduated from Maryville on-campus status and now attend universities on scholarships from Smyth, to crack cocaine babies no one wants, to temporary young guests awaiting permanent foster home assignments. The way Smyth raises money to pay for this extended family is even more staggering: a summer barbeque that brings in four million, a benefit concert and subsequent CD by Who rocker Pete Townshend that gains Smyth a million and a half, a yearly Chicago Blackhawk charity ball that raises nearly a mil—to name-but a few. And all from a man who holds the record for fouling out of basketball games at Notre Dame.

During our interview, I mentioned his *elbows*. "Back in college, there was one body part that people constantly mentioned when describing your style of play. For some players, it was the hands, others, their quick feet or keen eyes. For you it was always the *elbows*."

"I used what I had," said Smyth. "I couldn't jump. I wasn't a great shooter. But I got a lot of rebounds and loose balls."

"Ray Meyer said you had 'sharp elbows.' Meadowlark Lemon said you had 'mean elbows.'"

"I had beautiful elbows," Fr. Smyth smiled.

"A lot of your former rivals claim you were a dirty player, while you used to say you were just 'aggressive.'"

"Okay. So maybe I was dirty. If those guys still think I was dirty after all these years, I won't argue. It's like when the kids used to look at this facility and say 'Wow, Father! You must be rich to own all this,' and I used to explain, 'No, I'm just a caretaker. I really don't own anything'—but after all that explaining they wouldn't believe me anyway, so now I just say, 'Yeah, *I'm* the owner. What do you want?'"

"People believe what they want to believe," I agreed.

"The way I look at it, there is a fine line between aggressively going after a ball and grabbing it away from someone, and going after it and grabbing a piece of them along the way. So I'd just go for as many loose balls as I could, and let the referees sort out the rest."

Indeed, that statement somewhat sums up the Smyth philosophy of life, except now we'd probably substitute "loose kids" for "loose balls" and "God" for "the ref." These key words changed as a result of an incident that happened when Smyth was a teenager. Growing up in a devout Irish family in Chicago, John was close to his two brothers and two sisters, but he especially looked up to his older brother Michael.

Smyth was already a three-sport star (football was his specialty, and he still holds the high school record with a 99-yard punt) at DePaul Academy when his brother, Michael, enrolled in nearby Mundelein Seminary to become a priest. Smyth was happy the brother he was closest to would continue to be in such close proximity, and the two made plans to visit each other often.

"It was 1949, his first year in the seminary," recalled Fr. Smyth, "and Mike was playing touch football with some of his classmates and — "

Yes, it was over fifty years ago that a freak fall during a football game killed his brother, but Smyth can barely talk about it, and when he does the event (according to my wife, Jeanette) "sounds like it happened only yesterday."

"I was a goofy kid until then, and didn't really take life all that seriously," Smyth said. "Why it happened, you can't say, other than it was the providence of God. But his death changed me, and I'm sure it affected my decision to eventually become a priest," Smyth paused. "And I know he's pulling for us in heaven, because so many positive things have happened to me and my family since he died."

Despite Michael's death, Smyth's direction in life did not turn immediately from the playing field; if anything, he poured himself into sports all the more intensely. After high school, John accepted a scholarship to attend Notre Dame, planning to concentrate on his favorite sport, football. Unfortunately, a shoulder injury during his freshman year ended his promising gridiron career, but Smyth remained undeterred. He decided to try out for basketball instead and, after initially making the Irish hoop squad as a walk-on, he gradually worked his way into the starting lineup. By his senior year, Smyth was a first-team All-American, averaging nineteen points and double-digit rebounds a game. Of course, some opposing coaches claimed he had never actually given up football, citing the fact that Smyth was whistled for 101 fouls in 28 games, but others craved his kamikaze style of play, including the National Basketball Association's St. Louis Hawks, who made him their top draft pick in 1957. With his basketball skills peaking at the right time, a hoop career seemed the obvious choice to everyone but Smyth himself.

"After my senior year at Notre Dame, I was already leaning toward becoming a priest," Smyth explained. "I had told the Hawks not to draft me, but they went ahead and picked me anyway. I guess they wanted me to be Bob Pettit's bodyguard, to keep other teams from roughing him up and to share the rebounding load." But if Smyth's mouth said "no," his elbows seemed to be, at the very least, saying "maybe," for he signed up to play on the prestigious College All-Stars vs. Harlem Globetrotters tour after graduating from Notre Dame—and he literally took the tour by storm.

"Back then, the Globetrotters were not only entertaining, but a legitimate basketball team, probably as good as any in the NBA," explained 1957 All-Star coach Ray Meyer, pleased as punch to have Smyth on *his* team for a change, instead of beating up on the DePaul Blue Demons. Smyth, usually assigned to guard Globetrotter legend Meadowlark Lemon, played great, becoming even more dominant as the tour went on. Smyth was named the tour's most valuable player at its conclusion, and even Meadowlark, the usual star of the show, agreed with this assessment, calling Smyth "the strongest man he had ever played against."

Meanwhile, the Hawks were practically begging Smyth to come to St. Louis, saying he owed it to himself to at least visit the city. Smyth thought hard about the Hawks' offer but, in the end, felt it still didn't offer as much as the career his late brother had chosen nearly a decade before. John said one more final "no" to the Hawks and to the world, and enrolled in Mundelein Seminary, just north of Chicago, to become a priest.

Although Smyth's vocational choice later proved to be inspired, it initially appeared to be a disaster. Unlike most of his classmates, Smyth had never studied Latin in college and ended up flunking the class. Greek also looked Greek to Smyth and, when he failed that subject too, his ordination seemed doubtful. But somehow, perhaps due to the intercession of his brother in heaven, Smyth managed to scrape by and escape Mundelein, and was ordained in 1962.

When Smyth was assigned to Maryville Academy straight out of the seminary, his initial reaction was relief. "At least I wouldn't have to deal with any more academics," Smyth sighed. In reality, Maryville was perhaps the toughest initial assignment a new priest could get. Maryville was in the midst of changing from an old-time orphanage with huge rooms, with thirty or more kids bunking to a room, to the modern model with smaller apartments and more family-style supervision. But the transition was neither cheap nor easy. In fact, shortly after Smyth was named Maryville's executive director in 1970, the Archdiocese of Chicago threatened to shut the operation down, rationalizing that somehow state social services could shoulder the burden of hundreds of unwanted kids.

Smyth also supported foster homes for those who were well adjusted, but after eight years at Maryville, he also knew that placing kids with criminal records or drug problems in regular homes was unrealistic. Maryville, he told the archdiocese, was needed as a "safety net." Plus, after eight years, he *knew* the kids, and that alone was reason enough to fight for Maryville's preservation.

In the end Smyth won, but his victory was not without casualties. The archdiocese kept Maryville—but cut off all direct funding to the academy. In time, a somewhat uneasy secular alliance was forged but, in the beginning, Smyth was on his own, scrambling for each nickel like it was the crucial loose ball in the waning moments of a close game. (Currently the Illinois Department of Children and Family Services provides approximately seventy percent of Maryville's costs while Smyth's endless fundraising brings in the other thirty percent.) And, as you might imagine, sometimes his elbows rubbed people the wrong way, as the following story from early in his tenure illustrates.

Smyth was already recruiting athletes to help raise funds for his operations, and current Chicago Blackhawk owner Bill Wirtz (as well as many of the Hawks players) were among Smyth's first headline variety sports volunteers. When Wirtz and several of the Blackhawks agreed to host the now-annual Chuckwagon event for the first time in 1974, the daylong barbeque raised $400,000—twice as much as the year before, and more than enough to catch the archdiocese's eye.

"Since Wirtz was the chairman of the event, he was actually holding the receipts," Smyth recalled.

But just before Wirtz was about to turn over the money to Maryville, Cardinal Cody (then archbishop of the Archdiocese of Chicago) called and said he wanted the money turned over to him. When Wirtz heard this, he was furious.

"Hey, I'm a Protestant," Wirtz protested, "and Maryville is nonsectarian. It cares for kids of all faiths. I want that money to be used solely by Maryville—without any middleman taking a cut!"

"So Wirtz called Cardinal Cody 'a middle man'?" I smiled. "What happened next?"

"Well, Cardinal Cody called up Bill's dad [then Blackhawk owner], Arthur [Wirtz]. Arthur was living on Lake Shore Drive at the time, so he and Cody were neighbors. After his conversation with Cody, Arthur then got on the phone with his son. 'Bill, the Cardinal wants to see you. He wants his money,' Arthur says. And Bill answers him just as firmly. 'No way! How do I know Maryville will get all of the money?' So the end result is, I go to see Cody," Smyth explained.

"And *did* you . . . fight him for the money?"

"Well . . . I have to tell you that Cardinal Cody always seems to get a bad rap now. He did an awful lot of good things for the Chicago archdiocese during his tenure."

"But you *did* . . . "

"I was probably wrong to do so . . . He was my superior and he made a good case for why the money should be handed over to him."

"But you kept it, didn't you?"

"Oh yes. Maryville kept it all," Smyth confirmed slyly.

And throughout the great growth of Smyth's amazing ministry to youth, sports always played a vital role.

Athletics flourished, with the young participants from within and the help of their older role models and donations from without. And it flourished because of the sporting good sense and competitive good faith of Maryville's main man.

"Did you pray before your basketball games?" I wondered.

"Sure. I mean, the team always said a prayer together before the game when I was at Notre Dame. But as for myself, I figured God doesn't care who wins the game. He doesn't care if I get the rebound or not."

"But He cares about everything."

"Sure. God does care about everything you do, and you should pray about everything you're involved with. That's why we offer so many different activities at Maryville, to get the kids involved in what they're gifted at. If it's sports, we provide them with the best equipment and opportunity. If it's music, we try to get them the best instruments and teacher. If it's mechanics, the best tools . . . "

"Do your kids also pray before they participate in sports at Maryville?"

"That's up to their coach, but generally I think they pray that no one gets hurt, and everyone does the best they can."

"Although Maryville does a great job trying to find the right activity for each kid, sports still has a special place here, does it not?"

"Sure. I think sports is a tremendous tool, and most of our residents participate. We've had a basketball league for the kids here for the past twenty-two years, and it's been very successful. Since winning and losing is a reality of life, we do keep score, but the main emphasis of our league is sportsmanship. So while we do give out small trophies to the winners, the biggest trophy—and the one we emphasize the most—is the one for sportsmanship. And it works. The kids really go all out to win that sportsmanship trophy. Even the kids we plucked off the streets behave in our basketball league. About the only things we have to worry about now is when the parents watch and get out of hand."

"As a priest, you surely appreciate the sacramental aspect of sports, how performing with grace on the field can help you gain confidence to do positive things with the rest of your life. Does watching the kids play sports help you evaluate them spiritually?"

"Yes," Fr. Smyth agreed, "and I think basketball is especially unique in that respect. In basketball, the players do not wear helmets or masks, so you can see their faces while they compete. And when the game is on the line, you can look into their eyes and get a complete psychological profile. At that moment, you can see the kids who have confidence, the kids who have no confidence, and the kids who have false confidence. And you remember these things, and it does help you deal with them as individuals later."

"Do you think it's still possible for the professional athlete to have this sacramental view of sports, given the big money they earn?"

"I think sports can still be that way for today's players . . . if they approach it properly," Smyth said. "If they realize the impact they have on the youth, and approach sports as a means to an end. And if they use their money wisely, use it to help other people."

"A lot of athletes do give their time, and many have their own charities," I commented.

Smyth shook his head. "You have to realize that most big-time pro athletes make enough money in four years to retire comfortably for the rest of their lives. God gave them these talents and they have to realize the money they reap from sports is primarily a gift from God. It's not enough for someone who has earned millions of dollars to give a little money to charity but use ninety percent of it to support a luxurious lifestyle."

I thought for a second. Father Smyth's suggestion that rich athletes do more than just tithe—a sound gospel-based discipline—still seemed a bit radical. "You personally still spend a lot of your time fundraising, don't you, Father?"

"I sure do. I hate it, but it's necessary. We've just taken over a new hospital facility . . . and I'm personally sending 148 Maryville kids through college . . . "

"I know a heck of a lot of athletes help Maryville, but if they all chipped in what they really could afford, you wouldn't have to fundraise so much, if at all. You could spend all your free time with the kids."

Father Smyth put his cigarette down long enough to truly consider the heavenly possibility. "Wouldn't that be great," he sighed.

◊   ◊   ◊

The building, a replica of Thomas Jefferson's Monticello, is perhaps the most architecturally impressive structure on Maryville's main campus. For years, Smyth has lived in a single upstairs room, refusing to use the spacious main floor for his own comfort. "Some of my [Notre Dame] classmates saw me living in one room, and donated a bunch of money so I could have a house built for myself. I told them that I needed a new house like a hole in the head, and spent the money on other projects." Still, if Smyth wasn't going to use those five splendid rooms for himself, what would he use them for? Using such space for storage seemed wasteful, while filling Smyth's downstairs with orphans was impossible . . . or was it?

In the early '90s, Mike Ditka's restaurant met its demise, and without a powerful "lead-in," the nightclub's next-door neighbor, the Chicago Sports Hall of Fame, closed its doors as well. The Hall's 228 members had no home, as all the various items of memorabilia were thrown into a huge storage locker in the bowels of Soldier Field. But when this lakefront stadium was refurbished for the 1994 season, the locker's contents were emptied and its members were out on the street.

It was at this point that George Connor, former Notre Dame All-American and Chicago Bear All-Pro—not to mention a member of the Chicago Sports Hall of Fame— approached Smyth. Would Father (himself a Chicago Sports Hall of Famer) consider relocating the Hall of Fame on his grounds or, more specifically, in his own house? Connor knew Smyth had a hard time turning away orphans and, with the eyes of over two hundred plaques— not to mention a 2,200-pound statue of Walter Payton— staring at and pleading with him, Smyth could hardly say no. Now, four years later, their frames not only call Maryville home, but these sacramental sports heroes return the favor by doing something their live counterparts don't do enough of—raise money for Smyth.

"It wasn't easy," said Ray Kavanagh, current caretaker of the Hall. "A lot of the memorabilia was either damaged, misplaced, or stolen, but eventually we got it together." Of course, since all the Hall's labor is done on a voluntary basis, it still needs work. For example, some of the old plaques need new names, and the 1999 inductees, including *Champion of Faith*'s Cammi Granato, still aren't up, even four months after the ceremony. Kavanagh, though, is quick to add that the Chicago Hall—with the help of Fr. Smyth's networking genius—is one of the few sports halls of fame in the twenty-first century that turns a profit. "The main thing Fr. Smyth has done is turn the yearly induction ceremonies into a huge fundraiser for Maryville. This one night alone puts the Chicago Hall over the top for the whole year. The second thing he did is change its name from the 'Chicago' to the 'Chicago-*land*' Sports Hall of Fame."

"Chicago-*land*? Why did he add the *land*?" I wondered.

"Because by doing so, Fr. Smyth could add Notre Dame athletes to the Hall, which is always good for a lot of donations."

"Notre Dame?" I exclaimed. "That's in Chicago-*land*?"

"You know. That far-*eastern* suburb," Ray winked, as I returned his knowing Domer smile.

◇　　◇　　◇

"I've read that, with all the tragic cases that come through here, you, despite Maryville's great success, still get discouraged nearly every day," I said.

"Yes, I do," Father confirmed, taking a longer than usual drag on his ever-present Marlboro. "There have always been the sad cases of kids from broken homes. But now with the abundance of crack cocaine, their plight is more tragic because crack is so addictive and now so easy to get."

"And yet, I bet people give you a harder time for smoking cigarettes than the average pusher gets for dealing," I noted.

"That's right. If I tried to light up one of these at O'Hare [Airport], I'd have ten cops on me in no time. But if someone's dealing crack in the corner of the airport, you're lucky if the security guards even notice. Cigarettes are not good when they become an addiction, because addictions override God. But I sometimes think our country's heavy-handed treatment of cigarette smokers is used to cover up its failure to control the war on drugs."

"And crack cocaine is the drug . . . that's destroying the most young lives?"

"Back in my day, it was alcohol," Fr. Smyth said. "But bad as it was, alcohol took a lot longer to get addicted to, longer to destroy your health, so drinking ruined lives more slowly. But crack cocaine is not only a quick high, a quick addiction, but an easy way to make a quick buck.

And because a lot of kids in that area have no money and need that quick buck, it leads to a lot of competing gangs and quick deaths. I think crack cocaine is truly the devil's work, the sign that the devil is controlling so many young lives. And our national policy, our 'war on drugs,' has done little to control it."

I thought it all sounded hopeless but then I realized that, because nothing is impossible to God, nothing is hopeless to a priest, as long as he can transform bread and wine into the body and blood of Christ.

"With your hectic schedule, are you still able to celebrate Mass every day?" I asked.

"Yes, and it is one part of my life I am always thankful for."

"Do the Maryville kids attend?"

"Sure, if they want to . . . but I or my staff don't actively try to convert those who aren't Catholic. To those kids we teach Christian values, but encourage them to be the best at whatever religion they are."

"But wouldn't the spread of the Eucharist be the obvious spiritual weapon to stop the spread of crack cocaine?"

You could tell by Fr. Smyth's eyes that, while he at least partially endorsed my idea, he also had to deal with a sizeable dilemma in doing so. Maryville was officially nonsectarian; in fact, nearly eighty-five percent of the kids weren't Catholic. And yet, the prospect of the Eucharist, the body of Christ that feeds our bodies to do Christ's work, and crack cocaine, the surest symbol of Satan's hold on the world, doing battle was almost irresistible to him.

"If one of the kids does ask me about becoming a Catholic, I don't personally teach them. I think the Department of Children and Family Services would consider that as using undue influence. But if they are sincere, I can send them to St. Emily's [the nearest Catholic parish]." How many Smyth has actually sent through the halls of St. Emily's shall, for the time being, go unreported—but if Father's love of his vocation is any indication, the numbers are significant.

Because, despite his daily sadness at the plight of many of his charges, the joy Fr. Smyth derives from being in a position to change their lives is even stronger, for his confidence in his collar is complete. "The only reason I've been here thirty-eight years is because no one else wants me," Smyth joked, but even the youngest of residents knows there is more to the story than that. Smyth combines a profound love of youth with an uncanny knack for dealing with authority (not to mention an unparalleled ability to raise funds). Still, he says he never could do it unless he was Catholic—and single.

"I sometimes look at my contemporaries who went into sports," Smyth says while glancing at a picture of Holtz. "You know Lou?" he asked.

"Yes. I've interviewed him a couple of times before, and I'm going to talk to him again for this book. Is there anything you want me to tell him?"

"Tell him I wish him the best. That [the University of South Carolina] is gonna be a tough program to turn around, but if anyone can do it, it's Lou. Still, I think those guys are nuts to go into coaching. All those hours away from your family are tough on your wife and kids. Now, if I'm out working on something and only get a few hours of sleep [which apparently is the norm rather than the exception], the only one I'm cheating is myself. Of course, when I do sleep, I sleep like I'm stabbed."

Smyth is sixty-five now, and while the end may not be imminent, he realizes it is getting nearer. "As more and more kids graduate from Maryville, I get more and more requests for weddings and baptisms," says Smyth. "But recently I've been getting a lot more requests for funerals. And most of these have been priests." Like the founder of a great religious order who thinks about what will happen to his community when he dies, Smyth sometimes wonders about the future of his beloved juvenile haven after he has gone to heaven. On the one hand, Smyth is at a loss to say who exactly will take over Maryville when he passes. On the other hand, in the clutter of books and papers that occupy his desk, the one that seems to sit above the others is the paperback edition of *True Devotion of Mary* by St. Louis de Montfort. Smyth, like every one of us, will one day check out, but the Academy's patroness is not going anywhere.

Perhaps the Virgin is the reason that peace always overcomes Father's worries, and his courage is always stronger than his discouragement. For, God Himself has given John a glimpse of what happens wherever evil attacks good at Maryville.

"Back in the summer of 1976," he explains, "I was downtown [Chicago] giving a talk . . . "

"For fundraising?"

"Yeah. With me, the two are rarely separated. But it turned out that a lot of the neighborhood toughs [from the Des Plaines area] resented the fact that all those minorities [who reside in Maryville] were taking over 'their' town, and they took advantage of my absence by storming the grounds with ten carloads of kids—and a few adults."

"What was their plan?"

"They were planning on starting a race war. They actually thought they could take over the place—or at least our teen dorms."

"And . . . what happened?"

"Our kids sized up the situation right away and mobilized immediately. No one argued, everyone went right to work. Our guys knew the lay of the land, so basically they attacked the invaders from behind doors and walls, and kept hitting them when and where they weren't expecting it."

"Did your guys call for help?"

"Yes, but by the time the police arrived, our guys had the situation under control. They had beaten these kids so decisively that there was nothing much for the police to do but round up the neighborhood kids and take them away."

"Is that when you got back from Chicago?"

"Yeah. I returned a little after the police arrived. Heck, even the police were laughing at how bad these kids got beat. Remember, our kids were from the streets of Chicago. They *knew* how to fight."

"I guess so," I laughed.

"Also, none of our kids were arrested and we had very few injuries, something I was quite grateful for," Smyth continued.

"Were you proud of them?"

"Damn right I was. And it was at that point I realized that I could not only trust the kids, but that I didn't have to worry about Maryville when I left."

I paused. "Saint Augustine was the first to write about what constituted a just war. Would you consider the Maryville Defensive a just war?"

Smyth laughed. "In my opinion it was, Tom. If *ever* there was a just war—that one was it."

2. Learning from Lenny

The Radical Peace of Coach Wilkens

Catholicism has never been a religious faith that has called for anything less than the best in people.

—from *The Good Enough Catholic*
by Paul Wilkes

I still remember the first time I talked to Lenny Wilkens.

"Hello?" The calm voice I was familiar with from countless TV interviews had actually picked up the receiver himself.

"Hello, Lenny, I mean, Coach! It's an honor to talk to you. I know your media agent scheduled me for only ten minutes, but if there's any way I could interview you a little bit longer . . . "

"I do have something to do in about ten minutes."

"Oh . . . I understand," I stammered, already beginning to talk faster in an attempt to get all my questions in.

"I have to change my granddaughter's diaper. But if you call back in about fifteen minutes, Tom, you can have as much time as you like."

I guess that statement pretty much set the tone—for this and all subsequent discussions with the National Basketball Association's all-time "winningest" coach. While most would guess that a man who recorded over

17,000 points and 7,000 assists as a Hall of Fame player and then amassed over 1,100 victories as a Hall of Fame coach would be too preoccupied with basketball business to concern himself with changing a diaper, the time he spends with his granddaughter is what he enjoys the most, and is a big part of the peaceful beauty of Lenny Wilkens' hard-earned faith.

Leonard Randolph Wilkens, Jr., was born and raised in the worst part of Brooklyn to a loving African American father and a white, devoutly Catholic, Irish mother. Lenny was barely five years old when his dad died of a bleeding ulcer, and he became the "man of the family." While his mother, Henrietta, immediately went to work part time in a candy factory, Lenny waited until he was seven to get his first job, delivering groceries. Wilkens later went on to work stints stocking shelves, washing floors, tarring roofs, painting houses, and loading sugar trucks before settling into a career as All-Star point guard. "My mother didn't like anyone who was lazy, and she would not let us be," Wilkens recalled, but it was his first job that allowed him to meet his first big role model—a man who, in being first, was perhaps the greatest role model sports ever had.

Jackie Robinson had just broken the color line in baseball when fate found his young fan Lenny—unbeknownst to Wilkens—making a delivery to Robinson's apartment. "I had no idea it was his apartment," Wilkens explained, "until he opened the door and I looked up and saw that it was Jackie."

"Do you remember what you said?" I inquired.

"Not much!" Wilkens recalled. "I was pretty stunned. But Jackie was great. He immediately thanked me for the groceries, then sat me down and asked if I ever got a chance to go to Dodger games. I told him that my brother and I would save up our money and when we had enough, we'd go sit in the bleachers. I'm sure Jackie knew that every kid in Brooklyn did the same thing, but he took the time to sit down and listen to me—and by doing so made me feel important and became my role model. I saw the harsh way he was treated on the field, yet he never complained. So when things went wrong for me or I was mistreated, I'd tell myself that if Jackie didn't complain about his situation, then I certainly couldn't complain about mine."

Still, while a baseball hero is no substitute for a full-time father, Wilkens' one personal encounter with Robinson had a profound impact on his life. For example, to this day Lenny rarely signs autographs, explaining that he'd rather "spend time with kids personally, because when their faces light up and you see them smile, then you know you've made a difference." Although Henrietta never remarried, Wilkens was fortunate to find the next best thing: their pastor, Fr. Thomas Mannion. Father Mannion sensed leadership qualities in the scrawny youth, recruiting Lenny not only as an altar boy at Holy Rosary Parish, but for the Catholic Youth Organization basketball leagues Father helped form in the neighborhood. In many ways Mannion was a father to Wilkens, not only helping the struggling family with food and clothing, but befriending Lenny with countless words of encouragement.

"While I never actually thought of straying from the Catholic faith while growing up, I became disillusioned many times, because the prejudice was so rampant and no one was speaking out," Wilkens recalled. "On the streets I was called 'half-breed' and much worse, but even in the Catholic churches outside our neighborhood, my family were treated as outcasts and made to feel unwelcome. I'd get angry, and a lot of kids I knew in the neighborhood got angry, joined gangs, and did not survive. But Fr. Mannion would not let me give in to my anger, and would not let me give up. He explained to me that God gave everyone free will to do good or evil, and made me realize I could not indict God for the actions of some of his people. And, when he saw prejudice, Fr. Tom would speak out."

And so, stirred by the memory of Robinson and the presence of Mannion, Wilkens' "game" grew. Initially deemed too small by his coach at Boys High School in Brooklyn, Wilkens undauntedly dedicated himself to CYO and New York City playground ball, where, he said, "You *had* to win, because if you won you stayed on, but if you lost you sometimes wouldn't get back on the court the rest of the afternoon." The CYO games didn't hurt either, especially those attended by Fr. Tom. "Everyone respected him," Wilkens said of his old priestly mentor. "On Sunday nights Father would host dances at Holy Rosary and everyone came, even the kids who weren't Catholic. Generally in those days you learned to stay in your own neighborhood, your own turf, or risk getting beat up. But for some reason, the kids who were athletes were able to travel from neighborhood to neighborhood and were left alone. I think respect for Fr. Mannion had something to do with that, too."

Finally, by his senior year, Wilkens wouldn't be denied, and the slight point guard averaged fourteen points a game on the high school team. Still, with only one year as a Boys High starter, it looked pretty dubious when Fr. Mannion wrote the athletic director at Providence College and requested a full scholarship for his young friend. In fact, the priests at Providence initially refused him, but when one of them saw Wilkens score 36 and win the most valuable player award in a prestigious New York City summer tournament final, they changed their minds. "I guess that one game pretty much changed my life," Wilkens said knowingly.

While the majority of his four years at Providence was filled with fond memories, as one of only six blacks in the 1,200-member student body, there were bound to be some bumps on the road. One priest, French teacher Fr. Raymond B. St. George, became Wilkens' new confidant. Father St. George not only attended many of his games and answered many of Lenny's questions but also instilled in Wilkens a love of opera music (which led to Lenny sneaking over to the opera house next to St. Louis Kiel Auditorium before Hawks games, much to the befuddlement of his Hawk teammates). Lenny majored in economics, and his teachers held him in such high esteem that they offered him a student teaching job, with a promise of full professorship as soon as he attained his master's degree.

But the late 50s were still a time of upheaval for blacks in America, and Providence was not perfect either. On one occasion, one of the priests called Lenny into his office. Knowing this priest to be a big basketball fan, Lenny figured he was being summoned to talk sports or maybe academics. Instead, the priest told Lenny to stop dancing with—and definitely not date!—the white girls who were invited to the Providence (then an all-male school) socials.

"What did you say to him?" I asked.

"I said, 'You're supposed to be a man of God. Do you think God sees color?'"

"And?"

"He kind of stammered, but finally said 'no,' so I asked him as a man of God, how could he make such a statement. And when he stumbled around and couldn't come up with anything, I finally just shook my head and walked out."

Wilkens also recalls being appalled with the choices for "race" on a form he had to fill out. "There were two boxes: one labeled 'Negro,' the other 'Caucasian.' I didn't want to check 'Negro,' as that would deny my Irish-American heritage and, besides, the 1950s dictionary definition of 'Negro' sounded more like an ape than a human. Of course, I didn't want to deny my African ancestry either." So Wilkens created his own box and labeled himself an "African American" . . . just about two decades ahead of his time!

And so upon graduation, Lenny ironically found himself with three choices. While none of them were particularly lucrative (except perhaps compared to those of his contemporaries who didn't attend college and stayed in the neighborhood), two of them were safe picks. The Providence offer was certainly prestigious for a young man from the poor section of Brooklyn. The second, playing ball for the Taper Tucks of the high-powered Amateur Athletic Union industrial league (while also holding down a job for the company that sponsored them), offered $9,500; not bad money for 1960. The last choice, playing for the St. Louis Hawks of the NBA, seemed the least logical. Despite being the Hawks' first-round pick, Lenny was initially offered less than the Tucks offered, and the league had so little prestige at the time that some still questioned its "pro" status. Having never seen an NBA game, the league held little interest for Lenny—until a Taper Tucks representative invited Lenny to dinner and a basketball game—a Hawks-Celtics NBA finals match-up at Boston Garden.

If ever a businessman used the wrong approach to lure someone to his company, it was this man that night. For not only was Lenny exposed to the best of the NBA, experiencing the electricity of a finals game in Boston Garden, but he realized that, although St. Louis had three future Hall of Famers, the Hawks didn't have a decent point guard. Thus, he could not only make this team, but he could start on it. Wilkens accepted the Hawks' offer after they agreed to include a $1,500 signing bonus to bring the contract in line with the Tucks' offer, and Lenny headed to St. Louis—although not exactly with his mother's (or the city's) blessings.

Although Lenny became a starter by the middle of his freshman season, life off the court was not so easy. "My mom was not happy with my decision to play basketball— not at first," Lenny confided.

"Why? Did she want you to take the teaching job at Providence?" I wondered.

"Well, actually she wanted me to become a priest," Wilkens said, going on to explain that his mom, like many pre-Vatican II Catholics, had been taught that the celibate religious life was somehow superior to married life. But she eventually came around; not only did she come to support her son's career, but he credits her with much of his success. "Never have I seen a woman pray as much or as hard as my mom did for me," Wilkens says. "Whenever I give a talk, I tell the audience that I am a testament that prayer works."

The racial fight was a longer struggle, one that Lenny still fights to some degree. After marrying Marilyn Reed in July of '62, the Wilkens' bought a house in St. Louis—only to find they were the only black family on the block. Wilkens' next-door neighbor walked backwards to his car every day just so he wouldn't have to look at Lenny, and not long after they moved in, a neighbor deliberately poisoned the family dog. Even at Mass Lenny experienced racism. "It was not long after the Church instituted the handshake as the sign of peace, and when I went to shake one man's hand, he pointedly refused. Well, I had a game that day so I was leaving right after Communion, but just before I left, I stood right in front of him in the pew, looked him in the eye, and said, 'You are such a hypocrite!' He turned *really* white after that!"

But God never gives people more than they can handle, and help was on the way for Lenny in the form of another new friend. The Reverend Dr. Paul Smith, the famous African American Presbyterian civil rights activist, moved to Lenny's street. One afternoon Dr. Smith went over to meet Wilkens, but Lenny kept walking away from him, backwards, mimicking his neighbor's behavior. Dr. Smith wasn't completely positive Wilkens was kidding, until Lenny burst out laughing. At that point, Smith laughed too and it was, as Humphrey Bogart would say, the beginning of a beautiful relationship.

Doctor Smith not only helped Wilkens cope with racial prejudice, but got Lenny to go on some freedom marches as well. At the same time, Lenny never forgot about his faith, stressing the universality of being "Catholic."

When I asked him if he and Dr. Paul ever talked about the differences between Presbyterian Protestantism and Roman Catholicism, Lenny offered, "All the time—and he'd agree with some of what I said. But in the end, it was kind of like someone defending their little piece of turf and, at the same time, being afraid to cross over to someone else's."

"Kind of like when you kids were in Brooklyn and each gang defended their own block."

"Yes, it was a lot like that," Lenny agreed. The difference was—both then and now—that Lenny was one of the few people who could cross over the line.

The time was now 1968. The Hawks had finished with the second best record in the NBA and Wilkens had finished second to Wilt Chamberlain in the MVP voting, but the Celtics had won the title again. Furthermore, Martin Luther King had just been assassinated, and the Hawks, although on the verge of contending for a title, were also on the verge of being moved to Atlanta, King's hometown and burial place. Despite the fact that Wilkens had the best season of any guard, Oscar Robertson was making one hundred grand, Jerry West seventy-five, Hal Greer sixty, and Wilkens thirty-five. Lenny demanded a raise. The Hawks offered a token increase, to forty thousand and, when Wilkens balked at their offer, the Hawks shipped their player rep, assist leader, and civil rights activist to the expansion Seattle Supersonics, and Wilkens never came close to an NBA title (as a player) again.

Lenny retired as a player in '75, but by then he had already spent several seasons as a player-coach—enough to know he had found a new career. "When I first started coaching," Lenny told me, "I'd get so angry with the players, so frustrated with their failure to execute. It was just destroying me. I remember one time in particular . . . I came out of the locker room after an especially painful loss, still seething. I was meeting my wife and another couple, but Marilyn took one look at me and turned to the others and said, 'I don't think we'll be able to go out tonight.' It was at that moment I realized I was not being fair. How could I come home after a two-week road trip and treat my wife like that? If I truly believed that the most important things in life were first God, then my family, and then our friends, I realized I'd have to change the way I looked at coaching."

"Change your coaching style?"

"To some degree, yes. I began to confide in my assistants more, and one of the older coaches explained that I had been a great player, and these guys just weren't seeing what I saw. So I stopped yelling and started teaching, helping them to see what I did." And, indeed, they did learn, as Lenny took a group of average players and turned them into an outstanding team. His '78–'79 Supersonics won the NBA championship without a superstar, as seven different players averaged in double figures. By keeping his priorities straight, Lenny became a great coach—but an even better husband and father.

In the morning, Lenny would pray, often at Mass, for patience on both work and family fronts. And then after the game, he would take ten or fifteen minutes to calm down, praying the rosary to help him leave the game behind. "The travel, the being away from home weeks at a time, is hard on a family," admitted Wilkens, "but you just have to make a pact with them. I'd promise that after every road trip we'd go out as a family for pizza or something, and then I'd spend quality time with my kids, one-on-one."

And so, while things are never easy for a man of faith, they do seem a bit more peaceful for Lenny, now that his kids have grown. Although he still spends his summers in Seattle, to be near his two daughters and two granddaughters, professionally Wilkens has come full circle, back coaching the Hawks, in Atlanta no less.

"Coach, I read in *Sports Illustrated* that the first thing you did when you came to Atlanta after being hired by the Hawks was to visit the grave of Martin Luther King [Jr.]."

"That's true," Wilkens said. "Although I didn't really know King, I always admired him and what he stood for. And I always thought of Atlanta as his town, so I wanted to go [to his grave] and ask for his help."

"It's just amazing to me, that just thirty years after his death, so few of the kids growing up in our country realize what he accomplished," I said. "I mean, here was a prophet who aroused great passion and animosity in our country and paid for his vision with his own blood—yet in my son's grade-school textbook, King is presented as 'a nice guy and good speaker who helped blacks and now has his own holiday.'"

"Yes, that is a tragedy," Wilkens agreed. "Our textbooks have to do a better job of presenting a balanced view of history. Plus, I really think they need to concentrate more on recent history, with the young, and leave the rest for senior high and college."

"Speaking of not knowing history, I read that when you were coaching Shaquille O'Neal in a recent All-Star game, he questioned your tactics, and when you told him that was how you used to run it as point guard, he responded, 'You *played*, Coach?'—unaware of your long, Hall-of-Fame playing career."

"Yeah, that *was* bad, but not so much because he didn't know about me. It's just that, without knowledge of those who came before you, it's hard to understand your place in life now. And to help them understand is a coach's job, too."

"You coach by teaching the players to see things a certain way on the court. Do any of them ever start to see the way you do beyond the court, to feel your faith?"

"I don't know if any of my players will become Catholic or Christian because of me, but I do think some of them have become more responsible citizens."

"You mean role models?"

"I talk to players a lot about that subject," Wilkens admitted, "especially with guys like Charles Barkley, who says he isn't a role model. I told Charles that *everyone* is a role model. Parents are the primary ones, but everyone is a role model to someone."

Still, while everyone may be a role model to someone, there are those who are role models to many. For example, Wilkens's son, Randy, models the Fourth Commandment: honor your father and mother. Although, at the age of thirteen, he infuriated his father by asking for hot dog money while Lenny was coaching the last minute of a crucial Sonic game, today Randy patiently serves his dad as the Hawks' information technology director. Marilyn, Lenny's wife, is also a role model. After thirty-eight years at Wilkens's side, she remains "as hilarious and outspoken as ever." And Wilkens himself offers us a model of faith worth emulating. Instead of sneaking off to the opera before games, he now looks for an open Catholic church where a quick visit before the Blessed Sacrament can help him get through the day "teaching, not yelling."

And so, when I finally hung up the phone with the NBA's wisest and winningest coach to make the switch from writer to father (and drive my daughter to art class), I realized I had but one regret: that Lenny could not be here in person to see my daughter smile.

Postscript

April 25, 2000: "Lenny Wilkens is one of the most decent human beings I have ever met," said Atlanta Hawks team president Stan Kasten, as he announced Wilkens's "resignation" after the Hawks completed the 2000 season with a

28-54 record, their worst mark in thirty-two seasons in Atlanta and Wilkens's worst season in his twenty-seven-year coaching career. "The Hawks were very good to me," said Wilkens, who did not attend the press conference but was reached in his Seattle home. "It's just time to move on. I still enjoy coaching, but I want to take some time off and see what's out there."

June 22, 2000: Retirement did not last long for Lenny Wilkens, as the Hall of Famer was announced as the new head coach of the Toronto Raptors today. After briefly considering an offer from the legendary Michael Jordan to coach his Washington Wizards, Wilkens joined forces with Toronto for a chance to coach the "next Michael Jordan," Vince Carter.

"You've heard the old saying, 'If you can't beat 'em, join 'em,'" explained a smiling Wilkens at the Raptor press conference. "Well, Vince beat us a lot last year, and it will be great to be on his side now." Kidding aside, Carter is the first bona fide superstar Wilkens has ever coached, so you can see why, at sixty-two, he would put off retirement just a tad longer to test his vision of faith on this talented but youthful Toronto team.

 # 3. Daniel "Rudy" Ruettiger

The Faithful Dreamer Who Would Not Quit

"Here comes that master dreamer! Come on, let us kill him . . . We shall then see what comes of his dreams."

—Genesis 37:19–20

For I am convinced that neither death, nor life, nor angels, nor principalities, nor present things, nor future things, nor powers, nor height, nor depth, nor any creature can separate us from the love of God in Christ Jesus our Lord.

—Romans 8:38–39

"Tom, this is Rudy."

He never said his last name. He didn't have to. There are still a few people in today's global world of sports who can go by a single name, and he is one of them.

"Hello, Rudy. Well, I guess you got my letter."

"Yes, I did. Tom, I called to tell you your writing is great—but I don't really have time for your project now. You see, someone else is already writing a book on me so I have to work on that project first."

"That's okay, Rudy. I understand."

"But, Tom, I want you to know that I really liked your stories—so keep writing those articles, okay?"

"I will."

"And maybe we can get together on your project some other time."

Rudy was right. We did find time to work on that project together . . . and the time was now.

It's been six years since I had that first conversation with Rudy—whose real name is Daniel Ruettiger—but in this case, the length of time is not long, but appropriate. It took six years for Rudy to be accepted into Notre Dame after he made up his mind to go there, six years between the time he decided he wanted to make a movie about his life before it was finally produced, and six years between the acceptance of the movie and the birth of his daughter.

Rudy was born and raised in Joliet, Illinois, the third of fourteen children (seven boys and seven girls). Rudy's dad, Dan, Sr., worked three jobs to support this mob (full time at a refinery, and part-time construction and pumping gas), and Rudy, for the most part, was expected to pursue the same type of existence. After all, getting a job at the local Com-Ed power plant seemed a pretty good situation for someone like Rudy Ruettiger, who graduated third in his high school class—third from the *bottom* that is—with a 1.77 grade point average. He certainly wasn't the college type, especially not Notre Dame, where he dreamed of attending. And although he started on the Joliet Catholic Hilltoppers football team, at 5'6" and 190 pounds, Rudy again would have been lucky to make the local junior college team—let alone play for the Fightin' Irish. And yet, somehow, Rudy not only attended the University of Notre Dame but also played varsity football for one of the best teams in the nation: the Irish. Still, you may say, Rudy did play only twenty-seven seconds of varsity ball and that would hardly qualify him to be in a book about star Catholic athletes and coaches—right? Well, you never would have asked that last question if you had just seen the movie!

Indeed, it was *Rudy*, the movie, that first turned me on to the great Ruettiger story—and to a lot more as well. When I first saw *Rudy* at the theater, I had quit writing and was working as a retail store assistant manager, paying the bills but not enjoying work (or life) very much. But when I viewed *Rudy*, it was as if a divine lightning bolt had struck me. I instantly realized that I could not give up on my dream of being a Catholic writer, and after the inevitable sequence of heartrending rejection slips (many of which I overcame with subsequent *Rudy* screenings), I began to get established and published. By the time I talked to Rudy again, I had published magazine and newspaper articles on everything from Catholic sports heroes to commentaries on the Eucharist and the papal social encyclicals— but this was my first book "deal," and getting it done would be one of the biggest challenges of my life. And when you have an "impossible" challenge to meet, Rudy's a pretty good guy to talk to.

"First of all, I want to thank you for personally calling and encouraging me when I started writing again," I told Rudy, catching him up on my writing "successes" since then. "I don't know if you remember the call, but it meant a lot to me."

"That's great," said Rudy. "I was glad I was able to help. Now this book you are writing . . . it's about Catholic athletes?" Rudy asked.

"Yes. It's all about how their Catholic faith helped them to succeed and the lessons their lives offer others. Your movie was great, but there were a couple of things I read about you that I wanted to ask about. One is how you said anger can actually be turned into a positive force."

"Sure. Anger can go either way. When I graduated from high school, I wanted to go to Notre Dame, but I didn't pursue it because everyone told me it was impossible. But when I kept talking about it, my co-workers would make fun of me, and my anger would become destructive. I'd go out to a bar, drink too much beer, and get into fights. But when I finally used my anger in a positive way, it helped me to pursue my dream of going to Notre Dame—not only for myself, but to prove to all those co-workers that they were wrong, that you can attain your dream if you want it enough."

"But . . . isn't it hard to be a Christian and be angry at people?"

Rudy paused for a minute. While he now makes a living as a motivational speaker, his strength is sincerity, not quick-witted comebacks; Rudy never claimed to be "clever." In fact, when Rudy enrolled at Holy Cross Junior College, his stepping stone to getting into Notre Dame, Brother John Driscoll found that one reason Rudy hadn't succeeded in school was that he was dyslexic. Finally, Rudy spoke. "Well, Jesus got angry at people sometimes, didn't he?"

"Indeed he did," I admitted. While most people think of Christ overturning tables in the Temple (see Matthew 21:12–13) when the subject of the Lord's temper comes up, I would guess that Jesus' anger with the devil in the desert (see Matthew 4:1–11) or his setting Peter right when he refused to accept Jesus' prediction of his impending death (see Matthew 16:21–23) is closer to what Rudy means, for they ultimately speak about someone trying to talk you out of your dreams, to take the easy way out. But there was another part of the story to Rudy's turning his anger into positive energy in pursuit of his goals. As much as Rudy fantasized about attending and playing football at Notre Dame, he did not realistically act on those dreams until the death of a couple of his close friends.

In the movie, the death of Rudy's friend in a steel furnace spurs him on to turn his dream to attend ND into reality. In real life, two close friends died before Ruettiger made his providential trip to South Bend. First, shortly after high school graduation, his best friend from Joliet Catholic, Ralph Girot, died in an automobile accident.

"Ralph was a kindred spirit—a fellow dreamer," Rudy recalled. "He was the first guy to encourage my Notre Dame dream." At that time, Rudy left the power plant to join the Navy for two years, where he met Lieutenant Mark Crowley, a Notre Dame graduate who not only supported Rudy's Notre Dame desires (even taking him to the campus after their Navy stints were over), but made Rudy realize it was essential for him to seek out people who push and support you toward your dream.

"Unfortunately," Rudy continued, "after the Navy I went right back to Joliet, and right back to the Com-Ed power plant."

"And right back to all that ridicule?" I asked.

"Yeah."

"Did you ever apply at Notre Dame?"

"I applied right when I got back—but I didn't do anything to give the application a realistic chance. Everyone knows Notre Dame is not gonna take someone with a 1.77 grade point average. I *did* sign up for some courses at the [Joliet] Community College, but I flunked them all."

"So it seemed hopeless to you," I said.

"I just didn't know what to do. I *did* know that if I stayed at the power plant much longer, the anger would have consumed me. Fortunately, I had Siskel."

Siskel was Rudy's other friend—and only true friend in the power plant. Some thirty years Rudy's senior, Siskel would sit with Rudy every day at lunch and listen to his dream for he, too, once had a dream to become a doctor, which he gave up when he married young and had kids. Siskel wanted to see that Rudy made his own dream come true. But one day after lunch, the feeders that shook coal down the conveyor belt kept getting stuck and, although Rudy told Siskel he would shut down the system for Siskel to adjust the belt while it was stopped, Siskel decided to start working on it before Rudy could reach his destination.

Rudy recalled the tragic event. "The conveyor belt vibrated and threw him into the feeders. He went through eight feeders before I tripped it up. Actually, Siskel broke his neck when he first landed, so he died instantly."

After Siskel's death, Rudy's grief turned almost immediately to anger. He was mad that his two good friends were dead. And he was outraged that he hadn't yet taken their advice to follow his dream and was still stuck at the power plant. This time, though, Rudy acted on his anger. He immediately quit the power plant and drove after work one day to South Bend, entered the campus, and didn't stop his mission until he found someone, anyone, who could tell him how he could get into Notre Dame.

"I knew that Fr. Hesburgh [then president of Notre Dame] lived in Corby Hall, so I went straight there to ask him personally," Rudy recalled

"Wasn't it kind of late?" I asked

"Yeah, I think it was nearly 11 p.m. by the time I got to Corby."

"Wow," I laughed. "Was Hesburgh there, or more importantly, awake?"

"No! Hesburgh was away. But Fr. Cavanaugh was there, so I talked to him instead."

Because of the late hour and desperate tone of Rudy's words, Fr. Cavanaugh, a past president of Notre Dame, initially thought Rudy wanted to enter the priesthood, but when he finally realized Rudy "only" wanted to enter the university as a student, he gave him a thousand reasons why someone of his academic and financial standing couldn't do it. Rudy, in turn, gave Father one thousand *and one* reasons why he *could,* and finally, Cavanaugh, convinced of Rudy's sincere (if foolhardy) determination, gave Rudy some slim hope. He told him that if he enrolled at Holy Cross (a junior college in South Bend also run by the same religious order as Notre Dame) for two years and got good grades there, he might get into ND.

Along with the plan, Fr. Cavanaugh later gave Rudy a hand getting in—but that was to come later. By the time Rudy met Fr. Cavanaugh, the academic term had already started, so the young dreamer had to turn around, go home, and wait for nearly a year before enrolling at Holy Cross. But this time Rudy did two things differently. When he got back to Joliet, he went to work at a construction site, to stay away from the naysayers at the power plant. And before he went back, he took his first of many trips to the Notre Dame Grotto (modeled after the world-famous grotto in Lourdes, the Notre Dame Grotto is a popular campus shrine for visitors and students alike), to give thanks for what he had accomplished and to ask for strength for the road ahead.

To most people, Rudy's dramatic late-night jaunt to Notre Dame probably seems ludicrous—after all, the semester had already started three weeks prior so he couldn't have gotten into school at that time anyway. It probably would have made sense to travel there at a later date (*and* an earlier hour) or just get all the information over the phone. But in the dreamer's reality, it was important that Rudy act on his anger that night in a positive way, and Fr. Cavanaugh not only gave Rudy's goal a direction, but attached it to a real person, a new friend he could fall back on.

Similarly, no one on their first day of classes at Holy Cross would walk across the street and into head coach Ara Parseghian's office at Notre Dame and tell him he was eventually going to make the Notre Dame football team provided he would be able to gain admittance to Notre Dame and try out for the team in another two years. But Rudy's impromptu visit *did* make an impression on Parseghian and, by finding out from Ara himself when the tryouts took place, he got that dream rolling as well.

Well, as those of you who saw the movie know, with the help of Brother Driscoll, Fr. Cavanaugh, and a host of others, Rudy was transformed into a student, and his grades became good enough to get into Notre Dame—on his second attempt. But whereas many people contributed to Rudy's academic success, not a lot of folks helped him in his run to be a Fightin' Irish football walk-on—save *Notre Dame* herself.

"Did anyone help you in your quest to make the football team?" I asked.

"Not at first. But initially, no one at Notre Dame wanted me at Notre Dame—not the priests, not the students, not the coaches, not the players." Even his father. "All my life, my dad knew me as the kid who did horribly in school, and he figured I was setting myself up for a big disappointment, for failure at somewhere we both loved. Dad wanted me to settle down, not crash and burn."

But Rudy did get accepted, and he did make the team, over a lot of guys who were actually more talented. "I just wanted it more. For them, it was a lark. For me, it was a dream."

"Now getting a degree at Notre Dame certainly has a practical side to it," I noted, "in addition to fulfilling your inner most desires. Was there any practical side of making the Notre Dame team as a tackling dummy, and being beaten to a pulp every day?"

"Actually, there was," Rudy laughed. "Except for the little money I got from the GI bill, I was dead broke. By making the team, I was able to eat [at the training table]. I don't know where I would have gotten money for food had I failed."

"You could have gotten a job at the cafeteria," I said, recalling my own student days.

"Well, if I wanted to make it the easy way, I would have stayed at the power plant," Rudy remarked.

But being a walk-on is one thing; actually playing in a Notre Dame football game is another. First, Rudy had to earn the respect of his teammates. This was no easy task, for the small, slow-as-molasses wannabe certainly did not fit in athletically. What's more, Rudy's skills were so far below the norm that some wondered if his walk-on stint was a publicity stunt, a death wish (something they were all too willing to support when the impossible imp would catch them by surprise and beat them on a given play) or perhaps he was just plain crazy. But when they saw that Rudy not only wouldn't go away but gave his all on every play—despite being constantly pounded into the ground by guys nearly twice his size—they began to accept him as a peer, and eventually as a leader.

Still, because the doubters back home did not see Rudy in uniform when they watched the Irish on TV, they refused to believe he was on the team. Rudy thus dialed up his dream a notch and, one day after Parseghian praised him in front of the team for the effort he put forth on every play, Rudy cornered the coach in his office and got Ara to promise to let him dress for one game the following season.

"I love how you described the importance of faith in tough situations," I told Rudy, referring to his book *Rudy's Rules*. "You talked about how you have to dig deep, but when you keep digging deeper and deeper until you've dug down as far as you can humanly go—without faith, you've merely dug to the bottom of a hole to find nothing left."

"I would have never made it through without faith," Rudy agreed.

"But in one interview you went on to say that 'faith doesn't have to be in the Catholic God I grew up with . . . I don't care if it's in a tree.'"

"You know, I'm *glad* you brought that up. That quote was also from *Rudy's Rules,* and it's incorrect. It should read, 'It can't just be a tree. It has to be in some Higher Power.'"

"But the Catholic faith is important for you. Isn't it important for others as well, those who want to reach their dreams?"

Again, Rudy had to pause. Like Fr. Smyth, he worked with people from many denominations, and wanted to make sure he did not exclude any of them. "Tom, I think people of all faiths can attain their dreams. The Golden Rule is the same for everyone."

"But isn't the Catholic faith helpful with people trying to discern their dreams?" I asked.

"Well . . . when the pope travels around the world and speaks to great crowds, a lot of times they aren't all Catholic."

"That's true," I agreed.

"And although he talks about Christ . . . doesn't he try to encourage those in the crowd who believe in a God but aren't Christian?"

"Yes. John Paul II often says that what unites us is greater than what separates us."

"That's what I mean!" Rudy said. "I tell people the very same thing."

Now, for those who did not see the movie, Rudy succeeded in fulfilling his football dream beyond anyone's expectations. When Rudy was left off the final Irish home game "dress list" (although Parseghian had promised Rudy he would get to dress for one varsity game during his senior season, he had retired and Dan Devine was now the head coach), several players went to Coach Devine and offered to give up their roster spots for Ruettiger. As a result, Rudy not only dressed and led the team onto the field, but he got into the game and sacked the Georgia Tech quarterback on the final play. Afterwards, his teammates carried him off the field as the fans chanted his name and gave him a standing ovation. Certainly, everyone (including Rudy) figured that was as far as his Notre Dame dreams could go, especially when he graduated from the university the following year, in May 1976. But everyone who saw the movie knows there was a movie—and Rudy was responsible for that, too, a second impossible dream come true.

Rudy, it could be said, is to athletes what Thérèse of Lisieux is to saints. If you list accomplishments (or stats), both had short and unspectacular careers. But when viewed in God's eyes, both the little defensive end and the Little Flower succeeded magnificently—and both, because of their humble obedience to others, put their stories to words (and in Rudy's case, a motion picture) and thus became an inspiration to millions. Saint Thérèse only wrote her best-selling autobiographical *Story of a Soul* because it was demanded by her mother superior, while Rudy would not have pursued *Rudy* if not for the fact that every time he got up to tell his story at a Notre Dame reunion, someone new would say, "You should make that story into a movie."

"Was getting the movie done any easier than getting into Notre Dame and playing on the football team? After all, you already had all that experience in dealing with adversity."

"No, it was harder," Rudy laughed. "First, I was trying to get the movie written by a screenwriter [Angelo Pizzo] who told me he hated Notre Dame and would never write another movie about Indiana sports [Pizzo had previously written *Hoosiers*]. Plus, Notre Dame [actually, university vice president Fr. William Beauchamp] told me they had not allowed a movie to be filmed on campus in over fifty years [since *Knute Rockne, All American* in 1940], and the Holy Cross order would never allow it again." But Rudy changed Pizzo's mind not only by his persistence—when Pizzo stood Rudy up at a restaurant, he convinced a mailman to give him Angelo's address and met him there—but by proving to Pizzo that sports movies are what he did best. Rudy then got Fr. Beauchamp to make an exception to Notre Dame's no-film policy by emphasizing the school's historical beginnings. Rudy reminded Fr. Beauchamp that Notre Dame was founded by a French Holy Cross priest, Reverend Edward F. Sorin, also a dreamer who not only didn't give up when his initial school building burned to the ground, but who actually took it as a sign to build the campus bigger—starting with a building topped with a large statue of the Virgin Mary! Meanwhile, the constant traveling that followed—from Hollywood to South Bend, and everywhere in between, to get the movie deal arranged—cost Rudy his regular job (as a new car salesman), and by the time the pieces finally fell into place, he was mowing lawns for an income and had $56 to his name. Fortunately, the movie by the same name helped change his fortunes forever.

"*Rudy* really was a great movie," I reiterated to the film's humble hero. "Just like with *Knute Rockne, All-American*, I look forward to watching it whenever it's on TV."

"Hold it a minute," Rudy stopped me. "Now I'm not trying to make myself look good—and I'm no Knute Rockne—but do you really think the two films are in the same category, at least as far as motivating people? I think *Knute Rockne* was fine, but I think it does very little for people who don't like Notre Dame or college football. *Rudy*, though, is about 'every man'—how anyone can achieve their dreams—and I think it is effective whether the viewer is a Notre Dame fan or not."

Rudy had a good point. In the week preceding my writing his story, a man at the YMCA where I exercise related how *Rudy* helped him pursue his passion to become a pro wrestlers' manager. In other instances, a priest used the *Rudy* story as part of his homily on Christian persistence, and an eighth grader in the religion class I teach cited the film as a true example of how to be accepted—and *none* of these people were Notre Dame supporters. Still, if you *are* a "Domer" dreamer, the film holds an extra special attraction.

"Even though the movie is aimed at ND lovers and haters alike, you had and still have a special place for Notre Dame in your heart, do you not?"

Rudy reacted as if he had been shot. "Of course! I loved it growing up, and I'll never forget the first time I went there during our senior year in high school. [Unlike in the movie, Rudy *did* manage to get on the school's team bus.] A feeling came over me like I had never felt before . . . I can't even describe it . . ."

"Was it joy? Excitement?" I asked.

"It was like . . . I was cleansed, like everything negative in my life was gone."

"You mean like sins being wiped away?" I wondered.

"That . . . but more like all the negative experiences in my life no longer mattered . . . You went to Notre Dame, didn't you?" Rudy suddenly asked.

"Yes. I was a student there for four years," I confirmed.

"Well then, you *must* know what I'm talking about!" Rudy exclaimed without saying any more about the subject.

❍ ❍ ❍

Although most of Rudy's dream, when I last talked to him, revolved around his budding career as a motivational speaker, a noticeable shift was taking place. Rudy and his wife Cheryl (whom Ruettiger married in 1996) were expecting their first child at the time, and I called back a bit after the blessed event occurred to see what direction the dream had taken, and I got the good word from the mother herself.

"How are you doing, Tom?" Rudy's wife, Cheryl, asked.

"Fine, Cheryl. I really appreciate you taking the time to talk, with the new baby and all."

"Well, I'm sorry Rudy couldn't be here also . . . He's had a lot of speaking engagements lately. So you're wondering about our baby? It's a girl, and her name is Jessica."

"How's she doin'?" I wondered.

"She's doing *awesome!*" was the reply.

"So, Cheryl . . . How has the dream changed since Jessica came along?"

"Well, Rudy has always aimed his message at kids . . . but now that we are a family, we know more about what they [the kids and their parents] are going through. I think if you want to love someone, it helps to know their experiences."

"Does Rudy do more talks for kids now?"

"Rudy has always done speaking for kids' groups, but yes, I'm sure he does more now," Cheryl answered. "But it's not just talks. Rudy has two books out for kids [*Rudy's Lessons for Young Champions* includes such characters as Rudy, the young eagle with a big dream, and Hacker, the crow who always has an opinion, most of which are negative], and this summer we're going to stage our first Rudy Camp."

"Rudy Camp?" I questioned.

"Yes. This camp will include sports and activities common to most summer camps, but will also show kids how to set goals and to stay on track to reach their dreams. Then there will be a follow-up with parents to show them how to direct their kids in a positive way."

"That's great," I concurred. "Now are you and Rudy involved at all with kids in the local parish?"

"Because of his schedule, Rudy doesn't do any regular volunteer work there, but he has spoken to the kids at both St. Viator and St. Thomas More, and when he goes to the Catholic schools, he always gives his presentations for free," Cheryl informed. Of course, to the outsider, that might not seem like much, but when speaking is your livelihood (and corporate speeches net at least four figures), it is something.

"Does Rudy prefer speaking to Catholic audiences, Cheryl? The reason I ask is that Rudy was hesitant to emphasize the importance of Catholicism when I talked to him, because he didn't want to discourage anyone from pursuing their dream. Yet, I sensed it was important to him."

"To answer that question, you only have to look at the most troubled moments in Rudy's own life," Cheryl answered. "When he was trying to get into Notre Dame, to make the team, to get the movie made—he prayed. Rudy always says he wouldn't have made it through those times without the Catholic faith—and he loves to witness where he can share that part with people, especially kids."

"What about public schools?" I asked. "It must be hard for Rudy when he sees a situation like Columbine happen and, because of the ban on prayer in public schools, counselors trying to solve the crisis with everything but God."

"Well, Rudy would agree with you, Tom, in that trying to correct something like Columbine without God is nonsense. But you can still reach these kids outside the school on a personal level," she said. "Rudy gets a lot of e-mails from public school kids, too, and he [personally] answers them with messages that include the need for God. Rudy often tells kids that even in a public school you can still pray silently to yourself, or if they find themselves in a situation they're not sure how to act, to remember WWJD."

"So . . . do you love Notre Dame as much as your husband does?" I joked.

"I don't know if that's possible, but I really do love the campus and the spirit behind the place," Cheryl confirmed. "Did I tell you Jessica was baptized in the Notre Dame log cabin church?"

"No . . . but I should have guessed *that*," I answered.

"You know, I've talked a lot about Rudy's faith. How about you, Cheryl? Is there anything about the Catholic faith that is especially inspiring to you?"

"It's Mary," Cheryl said. "The Virgin Mary has been an inspiration to me for a long time . . . but now that I'm a mother myself, there's a whole new dimension to my devotion to her."

"I should have known! No wonder you can put up with Rudy's love for Notre Dame."

○   ○   ○

I walked out of Father's office, stunned and defeated. I had entered the appointment hoping to obtain funds (from a priest who, in the past, had been encouraging about my writing) for our children to attend parochial school. Instead, I got a sermon about how I had not only set up my son for failure by allowing him to dream about attending a Catholic high school that was beyond his academic capabilities, but I had failed my family financially by taking a flexible (but lower paying) job so I could pursue my writing.

Maybe Father is right, I thought to myself. *After all, when Rudy pursued his dreams, he was single.* Besides, I was falling further and further behind on the deadline for this book. *Maybe I should cut my losses, get a regular job, and quit the book. Just quit.*

○   ○   ○

"Tom, my life changed forever that last Friday of my football career," Rudy told me. He was referring to the fact that he had, after two years, quit the squad one day before the completion of the season because he was not on the final game's dress list, and his dream for playing a game for the Irish had vanished. Of course, unbeknownst to Rudy, several players had found out about this and had sacrificed their own roster spots so that Rudy could dress for Georgia Tech. But here was Rudy, quitting the team one day before the season was over—until some friends, including a janitor, convinced him of what a "jackass he was."

"Rudy, you can't quit. This is your dream," the janitor said.

"My dream was playing in a Notre Dame game," Rudy sulked.

"Rudy, if you quit now, you're letting them *beat* you. And there won't be a day that goes by that you won't regret it! Now, get out there!" the janitor thundered.

"He showed me that playing wasn't really my dream as much as giving my all to pursue my goal. If you give everything you have in attaining your dream and it doesn't happen as you had planned, there is no disgrace whatsoever. But I hadn't done that," Rudy reminded me. "Of course, in the end, my dream *did* happen, but if I had quit, I would have always regretted it."

And so, once again taking a cue from Rudy, I fought against all obstacles (including typing the last four chapters of *Champions of Faith* on a public library computer when our home system crashed) and finished the book. My son, John (with the help of income he earned caddying six days a week through the summer), was on the honor roll his freshman year at a Catholic high school, and while we are not exactly out of the woods financially, Rudy proved to me that if you do your best to realize a positive dream, God will take care of the rest.

Postscript

Rudy and his wife, Cheryl, have now created the Rudy Foundation, whose mission is to "help children of all ages reach their potential . . . by creating programs to develop and enhance children mentally, emotionally, physically, and spiritually."

For more information, please write:

Rudy International
109 Weatherwood Court
Henderson, NV 89014
or visit Rudy at www.rudyint.com

4. The Mom Who Was Point Guard

The Story of Suzie McConnell-Serio

We know that all things work together for good for those who love God, who are called according to his purpose.

—Romans 8:28

Whether it is her faith, her family, or the fact she doesn't make the big bucks like her male hardwood counterparts, Cleveland Rocker point guard Suzie McConnell-Serio reminds one of the Catholic girl next door. Of course, this girl next door is now a busy mother of four, so I was especially appreciative of the time she was willing to give to our interview. But having been down that parental road myself, I know how important our children's needs and questions are, so I'm not put off by a few pint-size interruptions. In fact, I wouldn't have it any other way.

Actually, interviewing Suzie brought back memories for me on both family fronts. "You're the only person I'm interviewing for this book who also has both four children *and* seven brothers and sisters," I declared to McConnell-Serio. "Of course, you have three girls and one boy while we have three boys and one girl. How many brothers and how many sisters do you have?"

"Three brothers and four sisters."

"And was your family very religious growing up?"

"Oh, yes," Suzie said simply. "My parents were both strong Catholics. Plus we went to Catholic grade school and high school. So not only did we learn about God at home, we had Mass during the week and religion classes every day . . . I still remember how I loved hearing the stories from the Bible."

"Do your kids go to parochial school?"

"No, we don't have one in our parish," Suzie confessed. "Peter [her oldest] goes to religion class and our church does a good job with it . . . but sometimes I regret the fact he does not have religion every day. It seemed, when we attended Catholic school, that being Catholic was a way of life."

As you might have guessed from her later success, basketball also soon became a way of life for McConnell-Serio. She played in her first organized league when she was in the fourth grade and, before long, was playing on the boys' teams. Meanwhile, her older brother Tim always picked her first on the playground, passing on older boys because, as he says, "Suzie knew how to win." After a stellar high school career, the Pittsburgh native picked Penn State as the place to make her picturesque passes—and pass she did. To the tune of *If You Knew Suzie Like I Knew Suzie* (a song the Nittany Lion band often performed when Suzie played—or played as *she* performed), McConnell set a National Collegiate Athletic Association women's record for assists with 1,307 during her stay at State. Of course, there were no professional women's basketball leagues, at least not in the United States, in the late '80s, but McConnell was fortunate in that the Olympic experience was not long off. And what an experience that would be!

"Winning the gold in Seoul in 1988 really was my greatest experience as a basketball player," Suzie recalled. After clobbering the formidable Yugoslavia team 101-74 in the second round and dominating the Soviets in the semis, the United States was forced to play the vengeful Yugoslavia again, but Teresa Edwards, Katrina McClain, Cynthia Cooper and company all converted on just enough of Suzie's passes to a post 77-70 victory in the final. "Representing your country like that, being up on the stand and hearing the national anthem play, that's something I'll never forget," said McConnell-Serio. "I'm just so happy God allowed me to play."

When she came back home, little Suzie was a big celebrity—if only for a short time. She was voted the second most popular athlete in the Pittsburgh area—being bested only by the Penguins future Hall of Famer Mario Lemieux—and actually made a TV guest appearance on none other than *Mister Rogers' Neighborhood*.

"It wasn't really that big a deal," said Suzie. "I mean, the show is shot near Pittsburgh, so I didn't have to travel very far."

"Not a big deal!" I exclaimed. "*Mister Rogers'* is the longest-running kids show ever."

"You've got a point there," said Suzie. "Someone told me after the show that when you're on *Mister Rogers' Neighborhood*, you're on forever, and they were right. For not only do they still show that episode eleven years later, but people still call me up every time it's on, excited to see me, not aware that I was a TV personality."

Not wanting to go overseas to play professional ball in Europe, McConnell "retired" from basketball and, except for an occasional rerun of the *Neighborhood*, her celebrity status ebbed. Suzie did stay in the game by accepting a coaching job at Oakwood Catholic High School in 1990. This certainly was in keeping with the McConnell vocation; at one time six of her siblings were in the coaching profession.

More importantly, however, Suzie was starting a team of her own. By the time the 1992 Olympic tryouts rolled around, Suzie had not only married Peter Serio, but had given birth to Pete, Jr. The competitive bug was still biting, however, so Suzie figured she'd give playing the game one last try. "I hadn't been working out much since the baby came, so I figured at the very least, I'd get back in condition. I'd either make the Olympic team, or come back to my family in great shape. It was a win-win situation."

Well, to make a long story short, McConnell-Serio did make the '92 Olympic team, but without the same grand result. Mostly coming off the bench, she could not save the U.S. as they were shocked by the Unified Team and had to settle for the Bronze Medal.

"Did you expect a close game with them?" I wondered. "I mean, you creamed everyone else!"

"We sure did," Suzie laughed. "Some people thought because our games were so lopsided, we might not be able to handle a close game . . . But most of us had played together in international competition for years, and we had been in close games before."

"Did they do anything you didn't expect?" I wondered of the former Soviet team.

"Not really. They played a tough match-up zone, giving us the outside shot, and we just weren't hitting, at least not enough," McConnell-Serio said, summing up the 79-73 defeat.

"I know Weatherspoon said, 'This loss will leave a scar on us for the rest of our lives,'" I added. "Still, being able to go home to your husband and child must have made it a little easier for you than Teresa Weatherspoon."

"Maybe . . . but it was pretty rough, something I'll never forget. The expectations for this team were so high, which made the loss even more shocking and disappointing. You always critique yourself more when you lose, but after a loss like that, you really start to ask why. Why did this happen?"

"Well . . . why did it?" I wondered.

"Tom, I do a lot of public speaking and when I talk about that game—which I almost always do—I say a tough defeat like that happens so you can learn from it—and through it become a better person. God, I believe, has a plan for us, and these things all happen for a reason—and we might not even know the reason while we're here on earth, but we still have to accept loss and move on."

And so, once again retired from the playing aspect of the game, McConnell-Serio spent the next six years concentrating on coaching and her family, two vocations Suzie intertwined uniquely and successfully. With Suzie's husband, Peter (also a teacher by profession), as their assistant coach for many years, McConnell-Serio's girls teams improved their skills while witnessing Suzie's family grow in size and in faith. In fact, there was one night when the girls almost literally saw McConnell-Serio's family increase.

"I read that you actually coached your team the same night you had Amanda," I stated.

"That was unbelievable," Suzie recalled. "I was still more than a week away from my due date, so I figured I was safe. And because we were playing a tough team, I wanted to be with our players. So I rode on the school bus with them—although Pete drove the car just in case. Of course, I started to feel a few contractions on the bus, but when the players started asking 'Are you okay?' I said I was fine, because I didn't want to be a distraction." The game started, and as the score stayed close, the contractions kept getting closer. "Sure enough at the end of the third quarter, my water broke, and I had to leave," Suzie said. "The girls all gave me hugs, and I got a ride to the hospital while Pete stayed to coach the game. We won, and Peter made it to the hospital just before the baby was born, so I guess it all worked out."

"Another win-win situation?" I joked, as Suzie laughed.

"Do you find coaching a good opportunity to share your faith?" I asked Suzie.

"Absolutely. A Catholic high school is a great environment to watch them grow. You have them for four years, and you get to watch them go from shy, quiet freshman to confident, polished seniors."

"Do they ever ask you questions about faith?"

"Sometimes . . . but as almost all these girls attended Catholic grade school also, they have a pretty good idea about their faith. Mostly they'll ask me questions about life—and I can explain how their faith fits into a situation."

In the summer of '97, Suzie gave birth to their fourth child, but also witnessed the birth of something else she dreamed about but doubted would ever happen. The Women's National Basketball league began play that summer, and as the thirty-one-year-old mother watched the action unfold, Renee Brown, who works with the WNBA selection committee, planted the seed. "I was doing a speech when I bumped into Renee, and she said, 'Hey, if you can get back in shape, there's an opportunity for you to play next year.'" "'Play?' I told her. 'I have this bone spur in my heel and I can hardly even walk.' Well, I started training anyway, but it kept hurting and, in November, I had to take some time off because I was in so much pain. At that point I figured there's just no way I can do this."

"Did you pray about whether or not you should play again?"

"I had a lot of conversations with God," Suzie recalled. "But just as I was about to give up for good, the foot started to settle down. So I resumed training again. I think it was on New Year's Eve when I was praying that God finally gave me the peace of mind that it was going to work out."

Suzie did well enough in the combines to be drafted by Cleveland in the second round in '98. And she did not disappoint the Rockers' faith in her, winning the starting point guard job and leading the Rockers to a 20-10 record. Wearing the number four—a special code for Pete, Jr., representing him and his three sisters, as well as the four teammates she guides on the court—Suzie averaged eight points a game and finished second in the league in assists.

But in another category, she finished first. "You *did* lead the league in *children*, did you not?" Again the amiable McConnell-Serio laughed.

"Yeah, I guess I did. A few of the girls had two, but I was the only one with four."

"It sounds like it worked out great with your husband being a teacher."

"Yes. The season only runs from June through August, which is when he's on vacation. We just moved the kids down to Cleveland for the summer, and Pete would watch them when I practiced." She paused. "I would never even consider playing in a full-length season like the men [the National Basketball Association runs from October through June]. My family comes first, and I could never justify it unless it was during summer vacation."

"I remember John McEnroe said he came out of retirement so his kids could watch him play, and Michael Jordan mentioned the same thing. Was that in your thoughts when you came back?"

"I'm not sure . . . excuse me a second . . . Mommy's talking on the phone and she's on crutches," I hear a most patient voice explaining in the background. "Where were we . . . oh, yes, the kids. It wasn't the number-one reason I came back. I'm a very competitive person, and the love of the game prompted me to try again. But that is a bonus, and it's very special, especially with my son. The girls are a little young, but Pete loves to watch me play, and really feels close to me through it. But even the girls see how hard I train, how much I go through to get ready in addition to taking care of them, and I think it helps them appreciate me more."

"I remember reading one article in which you compared playing point guard to taking care of your kids, saying, 'My job is to take care of my teammates sort of like I take care of my children. There are similarities because when I take care of one, I'm also trying not to slight the others.' Does being a mother help you be a better leader on the court?"

"It's certainly made me smarter and a bit more patient."

"Sports are sometimes called 'sacramental' by Catholics, because they are both symbolic and have a real dimension at the same time. Do you ever think about sports that way?"

"Sure. I think the sacraments bring you closer to God, while sports brings you closer to your teammates and the fans. One thing I noticed through playing sports—if you feel good about yourself, it affects everything you do. So if you feel good about the effort you put forth in a game, you'll feel that much better about everything you do that day."

"Has your prayer life grown through all of your coaching and playing and, of course, mothering?"

"I think over time it has deepened. I guess you could say I have general conversations with God quite often now—while sitting in the car, before I go to sleep, just about whenever I have some quiet time," Suzie confided.

And McConnell-Serio needs a deep prayer life lately, at least on the basketball front. In 1999, Suzie missed most of Cleveland's games with foot problems, and the Rockers fell to 7-25. And just this winter, at a time when she was readying herself for the 2000 season, x-rays revealed another hairline fracture in her foot—and her basketball future is up in the air again.

"Yes, it's frustrating now," admitted McConnell-Serio. "This injury is definitely testing my patience, but I'm sure it's another lesson God wants me to learn. Excuse me again."

After Suzie went to tend to her children one more time, I asked her about her children's faith.

"You said Pete really appreciates seeing you play basketball. Is he starting to appreciate the faith a bit more?"

"It's funny you should mention that. Since his first Communion, Pete does ask questions more."

"Such as?"

"The other Sunday he asked why we go to church."

"And what did you answer?"

"I told him we go there to pray and to honor God in his home," Suzie responded. "We thank Him for all He has done for us. He died on the cross for us—I am on the phone!" I smiled to myself, respectful of the way Suzie had to divide her attentions.

"Does he appreciate receiving Jesus in the Eucharist?" I could tell, by the frequency of the child-inspired interruptions, that our interview time was growing short, but I was hoping to get a few more questions answered before the kids prevailed.

"He thinks about it a lot and I do think he understands it."

"When did you become convinced of the Real Presence, of the importance of going to Mass?" I wondered.

"It was at Penn State. My parents weren't there and so it was my choice. No longer did I need to go out of obligation, and there were a few times, while on the road with the team, that I missed Sunday Mass. And almost immediately I didn't feel good about myself. It wasn't the feeling that I missed something, but more like something was *missing*."

"How about the sacrament of marriage? Was that a turning point in your relationship with God?"

"I think everything that has happened to me in my life is because of God, but Peter is the best thing that happened to me. He's my best friend—the father of my children."

"Some of the athletes and coaches I spoke to talked about their championships, the way things worked out for them to be accomplished, as being 'miracles.' How about you?"

Suzie pondered a second and then answered. "These are my miracles. My *four* miracles." I could picture her looking around at her miracles, known as Peter, Jordan, Amanda, and Madison. Again McConnell-Serio paused, and then answered one last question, and in doing so summed up everything that had been said in that past hour.

"If you ever get to the point where you question your faith and wonder if God exists, all you have to do is look at one of these children and you realize that He is real. Nothing so beautiful, so miraculous, could come into existence by just our own power—nothing proves that God is present more than they."

As we said our goodbyes, I thought about her last statement, perhaps the most perfect one I've had with which to end an interview. Indeed, there was nothing I could add to it except to say that it was a declaration her old friend Mr. Rogers—and of course Jesus Christ—would have been proud of.

5. Bobby Allison's Race for Salvation

He has stripped me of my glory, . . .

my hope he has uprooted like a tree . . .

My breath is abhorred by my wife, . . .

The young children, too, despise me; . . .

I know that my Vindicator lives

and that he will at last stand forth . . .

—Job 19:9–10, 17–18, 25

Bobby Allison has always been a proud man, and he's always had much to be proud of. A beautiful wife, four lovely children (two of which, Davey and Clifford, followed him into the racing profession), and accomplishments of NASCAR fame almost too numerous to name. And although it wasn't as obvious to the average fan, Bobby is also a humble man, praying grace before meals and the Sign of the Cross before races, thankful for what he has been given and hopeful for what he might attain. But life has lately dealt Bobby more losses than wins, and the only thing now clear to Bobby, in his slow race to salvation, is that faith will never again take a back seat.

"We can start the interview in just a minute," Bobby explains to me, "but first let me comb my hair." At first glance, this statement may not seem like an unusual request. But when you are doing the interview over the phone, it does set quite a tone.

Bobby was born in Miami, one of ten children, to a dad who was an expert mechanic and a mom who went to

Mass every day. After graduating from Archbishop Curley High School, Bobby and brother Donnie moved to Hueytown, Alabama, where they opened a garage. Later, they both took to racing the cars they built, but only Bobby excelled; first in the short-track modified car races, and then graduating to NASCAR, where he often led the circuit in both wins and "run-ins." But constant crashes with Richard Petty and dangerous duels with Darrell Waltrip was kid stuff compared to what happened beginning in the summer of 1988.

"Life has certainly been a battle since then," Bobby admitted as we began. "I still hurt every day from my '88 injuries. I just tell everyone to do the best they can and pray I can do the same."

"Do you pray the rosary?" I asked.

"Not usually . . . parts of it," indicated the struggling Allison. "Sometimes I'll say some Hail Marys. Sometimes I'll pray the Glory Be. Sometimes I'll just pray 'God bless our family' or something like that."

"Have you always prayed, or mostly just since . . . ?"

"Oh, I've always prayed," Bobby explained. "As a kid, Mom made sure we said grace before all meals and dad saw to it we went to Mass every Sunday. When I got older, I'd ask God to help me earn enough money to provide for my family . . . and when I had enough money, I'd pray for something else [for them]. And just before every race, I made the sign of the cross. That was something my mom instilled . . . a gift she gave to me."

"How about Mass? With races almost always on Sunday, did you ever miss?"

"Never. You could go early Sunday, or you could go Saturday night," Bobby paused. "Or sometimes I had a priest friend say them special for me."

Father Dale Grubba, the "priest friend," has known Bobby and the Allison family for almost thirty years. After meeting Bobby in Warsaw, Wisconsin, at a pre-race appearance in the early '70s, he became a spokesman for the racer, especially when Allison couldn't quite make his own thoughts clear. With Bobby's blessing, I also talked with Fr. Grubba about Allison, his family, and his career.

"I was teaching at the seminary [at their first meeting]," Father explained, "and so with my summers fairly free of obligation, I got involved with NASCAR—saying Mass or invocations before the race, counseling the drivers, or just watching. I was actually doing a column for *Checkered Flag* magazine when I met Bobby at that Warsaw car dealership appearance. I asked him questions in between the people meeting him and shaking his hand—and I ended up staying the whole day. When Bobby's scheduled appearance ended, I started to walk away when he suddenly said in a sharp voice, 'Hey Father! Get over here!' I thought he was going to bawl me out for not being a serious priest, talking about racing all afternoon. Instead, he looked me in the eye and said, 'I want to go to confession.' That was the beginning of our friendship. In fact, I'm writing a book about Bobby, comparing him to Job." (When I told this to Allison, he humbly said, "I think it's an honor that he compares me to Job, but I don't think I really can be. I would have liked to have been as strong as he.")

"Did Bobby have a strong prayer life back when he was racing?" I asked Fr. Grubba.

"Bobby was always serious about his salvation," Father said, noting that Bobby continued to ask him to hear his confession whenever their paths would cross. "Even the little things, such as making the sign of the cross before races, meant a lot to him. In fact, Bobby would also make the sign of the cross each time he flew his airplane. And then, when I was with him, he would also bless himself when we landed, and then would look over at me with a sly smile and say, 'Cheated death again.'"

"Are you sure it wasn't just a good-luck charm or ritual he went through?" I asked.

"No, it was real," Father insisted. "And the reason I say that is because after the '88 accident, Bobby was in a coma for a long time, and he wasn't responding to anything or anyone. But when I asked him to do what he did before every race, he slowly raised his hand and made the sign of the cross, and that was the first time he showed he understood what was going on."

"Were there specific things you prayed for before the race?" I asked Bobby.

"Well . . . I'd pray that I'd do my best, and perform with the proper attitude."

"How about your attitude racing Richard Petty?" I wondered. "Ed Hinton in *Sports Illustrated* reported that you 'wrecked each other repeatedly and intentionally in races across America.'"

"I wouldn't say 'intentionally,'" Bobby said deliberately. "There was some contact as a result of serious, hard racing . . . Your car would slide a little bit over the line . . . "

"But even Petty admits to the mutual bumping."

"I would never start such a thing," Bobby stated. "Of course, I might finish it," he laughed.

"Did some of your . . . *rivalry* with Petty stem back from that race in Winston Salem in '71 when you won the race, only to have your car later declared illegal?"

"They said my car was okay before the race . . . but later they decided my Mustang was too light to qualify as a Winston Cup car, and then they gave the win to the second-place finisher . . . the King. Petty wouldn't have had his two hundred wins without that one." (The all-time NASCAR win-list reads Richard Petty 200, David Pearson 105, and Bobby Allison and Darrell Waltrip tied for third with 84, although Bobby says he has 85, "because I still have the Winston Salem trophy to prove it.")

"What about the time they gave Petty your Firestones?" I asked Allison about a popular racing story.

"I tell you what really happened there," said Bobby, warming to the task. "I had just started racing for Cotton Owens and was fresh off a win at Augusta, excited because now we were in Birmingham, which was my home track. Now Cotton's team was paid to use a certain type of Firestones, but I had some better Firestones for this track, the Red Dot 103s, back in my shop. So I quick send someone home, have four put on my car, and race around the track just once, in the best time at Birmingham ever. I get out of the car smiling, but proud I pulled a fast one, knowing after just that one lap that the race is a done deal. But just as I'm about to put the car away, sure enough, some Firestone rep comes up and says, 'Hey, those aren't the tires we gave you for the race! Take those off!' And you know who they wanted to give them to?"

"Petty?"

"Yep. But I said, 'Those are my tires,' and he says, 'Firestone only lent them to you—take 'em off!' I say, 'No way.' Now Cotton comes over, real angrily, and says to give them the tires, and we start arguing. And finally he just throws up his hands and walks away. So I give them the tires—but I put on four Goodyears just to show them."

"What happened?" I wondered.

"Well, I won the race, but Cotton fired me the next week."

I later asked Fr. Grubba if he thought that NASCAR, in an effort to build up certain stars, gave Richard Petty an unfair advantage. "There's no doubt sports promote certain figures over others," Father explained, "and Bobby was always making waves."

"Do you think it was because of Bobby's integrity as a Catholic Christian that he always stood up when sponsors didn't play fair, and that in turn was why he was dropped by so many race teams?"

"I think Bobby did have integrity and always stood up for what he believed in," said Father. "But I think some of it was that he was very independent, being both an expert mechanic and driver, that he didn't always see the need to work things out."

○   ○   ○

"Are you proud you won doing it your way," I asked Bobby, "with so many different race teams . . . or would you trade that now for more wins?"

"I'd trade it for the wins," Bobby said regretfully.

"How about Darrell Waltrip? I know you had a fierce rivalry with him . . . but have you finally forgiven him for his tactics or apologized for your own?"

"I have not forgiven him . . . totally. I might be shoveling coal with the little red guy some day for saying that, but no. I respect Darrell . . . he was a great competitor, but he was the one who always ran into me, and he feels I owe him an apology? Does Bill Parcells apologize to the other coach after he wins a game? I think that type of [gamesmanship] is part of what you accept when you are out there."

Later, when I talked to Fr. Grubba, I wanted to know what he thought about this situation. "Father, why do you think Bobby still has such a dislike for Waltrip after all this time?"

"Part of it is that they were opponents. When you get to the pinnacle of a profession such as this, I think you have to convince yourself that you are the best, that you cannot lose. If you don't win, the tendency is to feel you were wronged. In addition, I think that Darrell came from that 'I've been saved' brand of Christianity, that says 'God rewards me for my good life by letting me win this race.' Bobby, I think, took exception with that—especially when Darrell was winning more than he."

❍   ❍   ❍

The year was 1988 and, to paraphrase Dickens, it was the best of times and the worst of times for Bobby Allison. Although his most valuable player years of '71 and '72 (when he won ten races each year) were gone, Bobby was still cheating time, if not death, by being not only competitive, but actually winning, including the granddaddy of them all, the Daytona 500, for the third time at age fifty. And better yet, the person who finished second was none other than his son, Davey. "It was the happiest day of my life," said his son, fresh off being named NASCAR Rookie of the Year in 1987. "It's better than if I had won myself . . . he's always been my hero." It would have been the happiest day of Bobby's life, too—if he could remember it.

There is a lot that Bobby doesn't remember about that year, due to the race in Pocano that took place four months after Daytona. Some in his crew claimed Bobby was out to wreck Waltrip (they had collided the week before), but before that could happen, a flat tire spun Bobby out, causing another car to wreck him.

No one who saw the crash expected Bobby to come out of it alive. As it was, even after emergency brain surgery, Bobby was in a coma for three full weeks. Then, starting with the sign of the cross, according to Fr. Grubba, Bobby had to begin life over again—learning again how to walk, talk, go to the bathroom, and dress himself.

As Bobby's great spiritual willpower brought him back physically, he gradually realized that his troubles had just begun. "I had made over seven and a half million dollars in NASCAR, and a few more million for personal appearances," he explained, "but NASCAR covered only a small portion of my hospital bills, as did Blue Cross . . . I had a Lloyds of London insurance policy, too, but somehow that didn't cover it all either. I ended up selling all my cars, except my '77 Mazda pickup, all my airplanes—even my house."

But if the accident left his body and pocketbook broke, Allison seemed to become closer than ever to his sons. By this time, Davey was a star in his own right, but would often travel with Bobby and ask his technical advice. Meanwhile, Clifford had finally made it to the Busch Circuit (a sort of minor league for NASCAR), and Bobby actually worked on Cliff's team as a part-time mechanic and full-time cheerleader. Things changed abruptly, however, on August 12, 1992. As this father-and-son team worked together, Clifford decided to run a practice lap for the Detroit Gasket 200.

"Before he climbed into his car that day," Allison recalled, "he came up and said. 'We're gonna get 'em, Dad!' But on the third practice lap . . . the car spun out . . . it didn't appear that serious." But it was. A frayed shoulder harness allowed Clifford's head to fly forward and hit the roll bar with such force that by the time Bobby and Clifford's wife, Elisa, had run across the track to check him out, he was staring back at them lifeless. Clifford was twenty-seven years old.

Davey was thirty-two when, eleven months later, on July 13, 1993, he crashed his helicopter into the infield at Talladega Speedway. Davey did not die instantly, as did his brother, nor did he survive, as did his father. For all three, it was the same—massive head injuries.

"Davey was an incredible young man," his proud father tells me. "He was so focused on his career. Clifford was less focused, but he was also a good young man. He had to live in Davey's shadow, but he was just starting to come into his own. But everyone loved Dave. In the five weeks after he died, we got over thirteen thousand letters from all over the world."

Recalling this tragic time, Fr. Grubba noted that "the outpouring of support for Davey genuinely touched Bobby but the one thing I remember most was at the funeral, when someone came up behind Bobby and put his hand on his shoulder—and when he turned and saw it was Darrell Waltrip, he started to cry. 'I'll have to forgive Darrell at least half way now,' Bobby told me later. It was the only time that day I saw him smile."

A few years later, Bobby's wife, Judy, decided she wanted a divorce. As most of the family's big-ticket items were already sold to pay Bobby's hospital debt, Judy decided to sell all his racing memorabilia in estate-sale fashion to raise a little cash and to cleanse herself of the past. I asked Fr. Grubba if he thought there was any hope of Bobby and Judy getting back together.

"I don't think so," he said. "You have to remember that during his career, Bobby was not only away for the races, but would fly into town early to make personal appearances . . . So he would go long stretches without making time to see his family. That, combined with his accident, the deaths, and the loss of his life savings was more than Judy could handle. As a Catholic, Bobby knows divorce is wrong, and I think his failed marriage often haunts him."

○   ○   ○

Bobby's mother, Katherine, is ninety-three, still drives to Mass every morning, sells Avon five days a week, and believes that her son's survival of and subsequent rehabilitation from that '88 crash was a miracle. I wanted to know if Bobby agreed with his mother about that.

"She's right," Bobby admitted. "I should not have survived. A fifty-year-old body surviving a 150-mile-per-hour crash? Not one doctor thought I'd pull through."

"She also said there's some reason God had all this happen," I noted. "What do you think that is?"

There was a long pause. "I don't know," offered Bobby, still baffled by God's ways in his life.

"Do you think people benefit from seeing how hard you worked to rehabilitate, that maybe that gives them courage to carry on and not give up in their own lives?"

"Most folks are very friendly to me when they meet me, and seem to enjoy hearing me talk. I just encourage them to accept adversity and to try to do the best they can every day . . . but why I'm still here? I really don't know . . . My sons were both killed . . . my wife left me . . . I struggle every day with little things that used to be no struggle . . . Sometimes I think the devil is laughing at me now."

◉   ◉   ◉

It is late now and I'm struggling, too, struggling to write the end of Bobby's story. It's easy for me to say—as it was easy for Job's accusers to give explanations—that a second chance, however short, to reconcile with your two sons should be reason enough for your accident survival, but I am not the one who suffered through the two deadly separations. And although Fr. Grubba tried to ease my mind by suggesting that Allison's last comment was part of his sense of humor, I knew that at best, Bobby was only half kidding. The former racer was more serious than ever, grimly searching for an answer to his salvation.

When I fell asleep that night, I dreamed that Bobby was racing again. He was out in front of the pack, with but a few laps to go. But one car began to quickly close in on him. Driving the rival car was none other than the devil. Bobby's mind was not sharp, and Satan was at the height of his power and seemed destined to overtake his opponent. But just as the devil tried to pass low, another car snuck in to prevent the maneuver. This daring driver turned out to be none other than Davey, Bobby's son, once again young and full of life. Undaunted, the devil then attempted to pass high, but just as suddenly, another car came out of nowhere to block him—a car driven by Bobby's other son, Clifford, smiling as he did the last time Allison saw him. Now mad as hell (what else?), the devil tried a desperate high pass, but he hit the wall and his car burst into a pillar of flames. The Allisons finished the race, first, second, and third, and their cars slowly rose, as the father and his sons drove off into the heavens.

"Wow, that's quite a dream," Fr. Grubba said when I told him, while another Allison supporter wept saying, "Bobby will like this."

But what does the dream mean?

Postscript

In what was perhaps the most important triumph of his life, Bobby Allison remarried his wife, Judy, in a civil ceremony on July 3, 2000. After having scarcely seen each other since 1996, the Allisons were "reunited" when Adam Petty (grandson of Richard Petty) was killed in a racing crash and Bobby and Judy decided to attend the funeral together.

"We were [at first] uncomfortable together after so much time," Judy recalled, "but we knew we must put aside our differences and go help the Pettys."

"The moment they arrived was the moment the healing began," Richard Petty said. Realizing the NASCAR family needed them, as well as their need for each other, the Allisons remarried six weeks later.

"The Allison's divorce was only in the civil courts," explained Fr. Grubba, "so their sacramental Catholic marriage was still intact. They actually were planning on renewing their vows in the Church on the Monday after the 2001 Daytona 500, but when Dale Earnhardt died, they decided to go to [Earnhardt's hometown] Charlotte, instead."

Through the sharing of his sufferings, Bobby found not only his reason for living but the love of his life—again—as well. And as they sit in their last winner's circle, nobody is as happy as Clifford and Davey to see "Team Allison" reunited.

6. Danny Abramowicz

The Prophet
Finds a Friend

To you, O God . . .

> *I give thanks and praise*
> *because you have given me wisdom and power.*

—Daniel 2:23

> *But the wise shall shine brightly*
> *like the splendor of the firmament,*
> *And those who lead the many to justice*
> *shall be like the stars forever.*

—Daniel 12:3

Like his apocalyptic biblical namesake, Daniel Stanley Abramowicz was always a bit of an underdog. Both men faced long odds to succeed, and it was only with the help of their God that they did. In fact, the "moral" of the Book of Daniel—"that men of faith can resist temptation and conquer adversity" (according to the *Catholic Study Version of the New American Bible*)—is pretty much the theme of Danny's life, too. Of course, there was a time when Abramowicz rarely resisted temptation and it almost did him in.

Despite a stellar National Football League career, Abramowicz clearly never achieved the fame or acclaim of many of his contemporaries, at least in the worldly sense. For example, while Abramowicz's stats compare favorably in some respects to his faithful friend Mike

Ditka (369 catches for 5,689 yards and 39 touchdowns in eight years for Danny compared to 427 catches for 5,812 yards and 43 TDs over eleven years for Mike), Ditka not only is a member of pro football's Hall of Fame, but has had two head coaching jobs and has earned millions of dollars in endorsements, while Danny's name is barely known outside of the two states in which he has played and coached. Winning accounts for much of this; while Ditka has won championships and Super Bowls as both a player and a coach, Danny has always played and coached for also-rans. There is, however, one list in which Danny's name was consistently near the top, and not coincidentally it was the one list in which I happened to be most interested.

When I began asking colleagues about Catholic athletes or coaches who would fit best in my book, Danny's name came up more than anyone else's. And while I had the unpleasant task of getting ahold of Abramowicz shortly after he and the entire coaching staff (including Ditka) were canned by the Saints, Danny's conduct still reflected the team's nickname. (In fact, even the Abramowicz's phone answering machine message contained the words "God bless you.") Ironically, the only thing that Danny was concerned about was that the book I was writing would indeed capture his deep belief in the Catholic faith—fears I put to rest but not without some old-fashioned second effort.

"So what exactly is this book about?" demanded Danny on the day I finally got him on the phone.

"It's a book about a dozen or so Catholic athletes and coaches, and how their faith not only inspired them to do their best on the playing field and beyond, but also how it serves as a model for others," I said.

"That sounds good," agreed Abramowicz, "and since Claudia [his wife] and I are going to Mass at noon, you might as well go ahead and shoot."

And shoot we did; the type of straight shooting two can do only when they are completely convinced of the truth that the Catholic Church teaches. My best efforts not withstanding, Danny focused little upon his playing career, despite the inspirational storyline of how a kid with limited athletic ability from a small Catholic college went from being a seventeenth (and last) round draft pick to becoming a starter and All-Pro, leading the league in receptions in 1969 (when Danny caught 73) and once holding the record for consecutive games with a reception. As we talked, I realized that this was not so much because Danny was disappointed in his achievements while playing pro football, but more because he did not at the time use the game to glorify God.

"I really enjoyed playing the game," Danny told me. "Back then it wasn't great money, so most of the guys in my era played football for the love of the game instead of for money, and they played more as a team."

"A lot of players used to say they would have played for free," I said.

"I probably would have said that, too—*then*," laughed Abramowicz. "I'm not so sure about now. My knees, my back, and a few other things from my playing days still bother me. Your body definitely pays the price for playing the game. But I loved the competition and enjoyed the camaraderie. Even though I wasn't on the best of teams, everyone seemed willing to sacrifice their stats—and their bodies—for each other and the team. Now, with a lot of guys playing football as a quick-fix financial opportunity, many of them just play for themselves."

Certainly, having just finished seven years of coaching in the pro ranks, Abramowicz speaks from experience. And while Danny admitted the last three years "were very tough on me," he sees more positive than negatives in the New Orleans coaching experience because he now realizes it was all part of God's plan. "I feel that we have grown through this," Danny told me, "but I could have never said that about the past three seasons if I had not made Jesus Christ the Lord of my life."

I wondered if Danny had ever left the faith, or if he had remained Catholic throughout his career.

"I've always been a Catholic," Danny confirmed. "My parents were very religious, and made sure I attended Mass every Sunday," he said, noting that he also attended St. Stanislaus as a child, then Central Catholic for high school, and finally Xavier University to complete his Christian education—and of course, to play football.

"But did you keep attending Mass when you were drafted by the Saints, and later with the 49ers?" I questioned.

"Oh, yeah. I went every Sunday," affirmed Abramowicz. "Even in my craziest days [which occurred after his playing career when he was a Saints broadcaster], I still never missed a Sunday Mass."

"I'm sure your team said prayers in high school and college, but did you still pray when you were playing in the pros?"

"Of course. But in those life-or-death type situations, who doesn't? When a soldier's in a foxhole under enemy attack, he doesn't say, 'Mommy, help me!' He cries out for God."

"That's true. My dad always told me there are few agnostics on the battle lines."

"So, yes, I prayed. But when I prayed, I was a 'deal-maker.' Instead of praying that His will be done, it was always 'God, if you give me this, I'll do this for you.' I just didn't understand how to put God and the spiritual aspect of my life first. So while I did attend Mass every Sunday, how I lived from Sunday to Sunday was a different story."

In many ways, Danny lived for Sunday back then. Not only did Danny crave the competition, but the discipline of training (see 1 Corinthians 9:24–25) and the lay-down-your-life game-day mentality of true teams (see John 15:13) combined to keep a kind of Christian mind-set in Danny, whether or not he realized the sport (or the Mass, for that matter) as being "of Christ." Of course, he was not exactly a saint off the field. As most players back then, Danny drank, and sometimes drank to excess. But Abramowicz was too intense a competitor to let alcohol affect his play, and once he set foot on the field, he never took anything that prevented him from doing his best. Unfortunately, when Danny's playing days were over, there was nothing to hold his party side back and, as his drinking increased, his Christianity took a back seat.

As many former gridiron greats have found, it is difficult to replace the high of hearing sixty thousand fans screaming their name once they've hung up their cleats for good. Abramowicz stayed close to the game by becoming a Saints color commentator and, although Danny excelled in this gig too, it did not demand the same type of physical discipline that playing did. In fact, commentating tended to lend itself to the party life and, before he realized it, his drinking and his life were out of control.

"My dad was a fireman, and my father-in-law was a steel worker, and here I was making big money, with people slapping me on the back and inviting me over to their parties. I thought I was a big shot, and went from drinking a few beers to drinking scotch, and finally martinis."

"So you were getting drunk pretty much every night."

"Yeah," Danny confirmed. "If I wasn't at a party, I was usually out in the French Quarter." He paused. "I actually thought I was cool, that standing out in the street drinking till dawn was the manly thing to do. Of course, I realize now that any village idiot can do that. The real manly thing is to not give in to peer pressure and to stand up for the Lord."

"When did you finally realize the drinking was dragging you down?"

"I remember waking up one morning, looking over at my wife, and seeing the sadness on her face. I then walked into my children's rooms and took a long look at each of them. Then I went into the bathroom to shave and, staring in the mirror, I took a long look at me. At that moment I began to realize what had become of Danny Abramowicz, and I didn't like what I saw."

"What were your thoughts as you looked at yourself in the mirror?" I wondered.

"My initial reaction was something like, 'If this is what life is all about, it ain't worth living,'" Danny remembered. "Fortunately, the Holy Spirit stepped in at that point, because I suddenly said, 'Lord, I need help!'"

"Did you stop drinking then?" I asked.

"Not immediately. I called up a priest friend of mine and told him I had a drinking problem, but when he answered that he was an alcoholic himself, I said, 'Wait a minute! I'm not saying that!' But I finally realized he was right."

Danny went to his first AA meeting on December 15, 1981, and has been sober ever since. Still, something was missing. "I was sober but not serene," recalled Danny. "It was like the part of my life devoted to drinking was gone, but in its place was now a big empty space, and I didn't now how to fill it."

So Danny knocked at the Lord's door again, and the Holy Spirit answered by persuading Abramowicz to attend a Life in the Spirit seminar, where he examined the basic tenets of the Catholic faith in an adult manner for the first time. Next, Danny began attending Catholic charismatic prayer meetings and, at this point, not only was the void in Danny's life being filled, but his faith was finally "on fire." "I felt like Saul [St. Paul], in that for the first time I could truly see," Danny explained. "I finally was a Catholic not out of obligation but because I wanted to be."

Abramowicz, who is a popular speaker now on the not-so-lucrative Catholic parish circuit, frequently tells audiences, "When the Lord starts working in a deeper way in our lives, He gives us choices and opportunities to right ourselves." While in retrospect, Danny's career decisions turned out fine, his vocational choices at the time had friends and foes alike scratching their heads. Surely Danny made the right move to resign his broadcasting job to be free from the party scene it entailed. However, when Danny turned down a $125,000-a-year job selling control valves to accept a head coaching position at a Jesuit high school for approximately one-sixth that amount, it was a controversial move to say the least—*especially* because he was already in serious financial trouble.

"What did people say when you did that?" I inquired.

"They thought I was crazy. But I wanted to have an impact on young men's souls, and football was the way I best knew how to do so."

Danny coached high school football for three years and, while his teams went on to have a winning record (20-14), his biggest impact was undoubtedly in his players' everyday lives.

"The first thing I did was put a crucifix up in the locker room," said Danny. "And before anyone could play on my team, they had to sign a contract in which they agreed to abide by certain rules."

"Such as?"

"Things like no drugs, no alcohol, no swearing, no failing grades."

"What made you decide to leave? The money?"

"The money situation was tough but, more than anything, I think I wanted to coach for Mike."

That's Mike as in "Ditka," who offered Abramowicz the Chicago Bears specials teams coaching position in 1992 after hearing Danny's rousing talk at a Bears pre-game chapel service in 1991. "I had known Mike for quite some time before then," Abramowicz told me. "Our NFL careers had overlapped and we played against each other, and I had been paired with Mike several times in various celebrity golf tournaments. But it wasn't until he heard about how the Lord turned my life around that he thought about me as a possible assistant coach."

Although most men would jump at the chance for that kind of coaching advancement, Danny was no longer like most men and, instead of jumping, got down on his knees and prayed. "You grow close to young men when you coach them, and because you've made a commitment to them and they to you, it's always hard to leave a situation like that. But I prayed over it, and I felt God wanted me to come to Chicago."

When explaining the hiring of a coach with no NFL experience to the media, Ditka said with his usual aplomb, "I guess I could have gone out and hired someone who had already coached special teams in the league. But sometimes you need an infusion of new blood to your staff, someone gung ho who's a little different. Danny will not only give it everything he's got, but bring us excitement and energy."

This time Ditka was dead-on. Not only did Abramowicz inspire a kamikaze camaraderie among his special teamers, but he tried more "special" special team plays than any coach in recent memory—and for the most part succeeded. From spot tosses on kickoffs to flanker pitch-out passes on fake field goals, Abramowicz kept opponents on their toes and Bear fans glued to their seats during even the most redundant special team situation. Still, despite the excitement, Danny's Bear career was almost over in a year. Ditka was fired after the 1992 season, and new coach Dave Wannstedt did not initially express interest in retaining him. "He had someone else in mind," Danny told me. "I told Claudia that we'd better pack our bags."

But Wannstedt's choice fell through and, when he watched the film and noticed the improvement of the Bears' special teams that past season, he decided to give Danny an interview. "You spend so much time together under tough circumstances as a coaching staff that you want to make sure the person has substance," Wannstedt said. Dave indeed found a man with the depth he was looking for, a man who not only spent hours with the head coach at practice but attended daily Mass and Bible studies with Wannstedt as well. But after four fulfilling years (three under Wannstedt) in Chicago, a strange move occurred—strange, that is, for everyone except Danny. Abramowicz felt called to return to New Orleans, so not long after the '95 season was over, Claudia and Daniel packed their bags and returned to the bayou, and they did so with no job—or job offers—awaiting them.

"Wait a minute! You mean you moved back to New Orleans without any job lined up?" I asked again, not quite believing I heard Danny correctly.

"That's right," said Danny.

"Let me guess. People thought you were crazy, right?"

Danny laughed. "Yes, but as you have probably *also* guessed, we prayed about the decision. In fact, when we got back, Claudia felt inspired to pick up the Bible, and she opened it to a passage from the prophet Jonah, when it talked about Jonah being in the belly of a whale for three days. After that, we both felt it would be three days before we received an answer as to what I should do next," Danny explained.

"And?"

"On the third day, Ditka called."

This time, Mike, who had just been named head coach of the New Orleans Saints, was calling to see if Danny wanted to be his offensive coordinator. Danny, as history records, said "yes."

"Did you at least have an *inkling* that Ditka would name you his offensive coordinator?"

"Not really. In fact, when we decided to move, I didn't even think Mike was a lead candidate for the job."

And so as faith would have it, Danny and Mike were reunited again. "Everybody says Danny is a reach," Ditka responded when he hired Danny as offensive coordinator with no previous experience. "Well, it's not for me because football is football. I don't need a genius to run my offense, just a hard-working Pole." Sadly, this time the critics appeared to be right, because even though Ditka and Abramowicz doubled the Saints' victory total from the previous year (three to six) in their first season in New Orleans, their offense ranked dead last. The quarterbacks (a position that would plague the Saints in the duo's three years there) threw for only six TDs while hurling twenty-five interceptions. Ditka, who had his hand in just about everything anyway, vowed to become more involved in the offense in 1998.

Hope briefly returned when the Saints opened with three straight wins that season, but when they slumped to finish 6-10 again, Ditka and "D.A." knew that "DA SAINTS'" offense was in dire straits. Saints president and general manager Bill Kuharich asked Ditka to fire both Abramowicz and defensive coordinator Zaven Yaralian before the 1999 season, but Mike would hear none of it, deciding instead to trade away everything but the kitchen sink to obtain rookie running back Ricky Williams to spark Danny's offense. But when Williams, as well as Joe Johnson, the Saints' best defensive player, ended up injured for most of that 3-13 season, 1999 proved to be the end of the line in the city of New Orleans, not only for Abramowicz and Yaralian, but Ditka, Kuharich, and every other assistant on that team as well.

Beyond the fact that New Orleans never had enough talent at quarterback during Danny's tenure to settle on a starter (the Saints started three different quarterbacks in '97 and four in both '98 and '99), the reason for Abramowicz's lack of coaching success in the Big Easy compared to the Windy City may have been simple economics. As special teams coach, Danny was dealing mostly with players on the lower end of the NFL pay scale. Not only did they have more to gain monetarily by trusting a caring coach who expected them to go full tilt every play, they also knew the Bears lost little against the payroll if Danny demanded one of them be cut loose. On the other hand, offensive players these days demand big signing bonuses, and letting go of a starting running back or tackle not only costs you the services of that individual, but a sack of cash against the salary cap as well. "A lot of the young players today are brought up spoiled," laments Abramowicz. "From parents to coaches to agents, they are constantly told they are the greatest, and when they get here, they can't take constructive criticism. But if they can get cut without playing a down and still get a bag of money, why should they?"

They should because they played for a man who would lay down his life for them, just as the Lord did for us during His earthly stay. It is certainly part of the reason Ditka kept Danny around when management urged him not to—and even when Mike himself often questioned Danny's play calling.

"Yeah, Mike and I had our disagreements on the sidelines, and since this was during the heat of competition—and we are both very competitive people—our disagreements sometimes got pretty loud. I'm sure everyone has arguments with their spouse or best friend sometimes but, as coaches, we live in glass houses, and ours are seen by millions of people. But I always realized it was his team, and if in the end we couldn't agree, I respected the fact that we would do it his way."

Actually, Ditka tried to do it Danny's way at least for a while. Appealing to Mike's own deep-seeded Christianity, Abramowicz convinced Ditka that it was wrong to be deliberately swearing all the time, and Mike agreed to try to at least cut down on his sideline cussing. While Mike was not completely successful in eliminating from his vocabulary the dreaded four-letter words, the fact that he even attempted to is testament to Abramowicz's positive influence on him. "Sure, Mike wishes he could take back some of the things he says," Danny stated, noting that Ditka does apologize much quicker now than he used to. "That's why they make erasers on pencils. I just don't think people should talk only about his temper and forget about all the good things he's done for people."

There is a certain sadness at the way his latest coaching venture ended, especially for those left behind. "I pray all the time for the coaches who just got fired," Danny said. "People think this is a glamorous business, but for some of those guys, it is the second time in two years they had to up and move their families." Yet, those very relationships are the main reason Danny says, "I don't consider myself a failure in New Orleans!" And, of course, the greatest friendship he forged while there may have been with Ditka himself.

"Do you think one of the reasons God brought you to New Orleans was to help Mike Ditka with his understanding of the Catholic faith?"

"It's possible," Danny admitted. "Of course a lot of people helped Mike, and he helped a lot of people, including me. But I would like to think that God used me in that way."

"So . . . are you now looking to get back into football?" I wondered.

"No," Danny said definitively. "I really enjoyed my ten years in coaching; it was a great way to reach young men. But I'm going back into the private sector," mentioning that he had accepted a job with a foundation founded by his friend Joseph C. Canizaro.

"Would you give talks?" I asked, recalling a powerful presentation Danny gave on EWTN.

"Talks and seminars . . . things like that. Our main goal is to build people up through the Church. The Catholic Church was established by Jesus Christ, but there's a lot of people who don't seem to know this. And because there's a shortage of priests, lay people have to get involved."

"In this task of building people up through the Church, where do you start?" I asked.

"We start with the family," Danny replied.

"Ah, the 'domestic church,' as John Paul II would say," I added.

"Yes, you can reach out all you want to others in the Church, but if things aren't right in your own family, it does little good," Danny said.

"Will your presentations emphasize the reception of the sacraments?" I asked the former wide receiver.

"Yes, they will."

"In one of your talks you went on at some length about the sacrament of reconciliation, and it impressed me because very few Catholics ever mention it anymore."

"Well, reconciliation is a very important sacrament to me . . . and should be for all Catholics. I try my best to follow the Lord, but sometimes, as I said before, in the heat of the battle my competitive nature gets the best of me and I say something I shouldn't have. But once you go to confession, that sin is wiped away forever and you start fresh. I feel so much better after I go."

"Do you ever have trouble . . . with a priest giving you a hard time in confession for your sins . . . or even things that *aren't* sins . . . say, vocational choices?"

"Sure, there's always going to be some priests who understand you better than others," Danny said. "But you have to realize that while he's in the confessional, that priest is not acting as a human person, but as a representative of Jesus Christ," Danny paused. "In this day and age, many people spend millions on psychiatrists and psychologists, when confessing their sins to a priest is what they need to be washed clean of all their anger or hurt or guilt." His comment was so striking that it made me stop and think. While Danny in no way espouses the wholesale elimination of gifted Christian psychiatric professionals, he emphasizes that the often neglected use of this sacrament by those who are truly troubled is something that must be looked at.

"What about the Eucharist?" I asked. "The *Catechism of the Catholic Church* calls it the 'sum and summary of our faith.' What aspects of the Blessed Sacrament do you like to emphasize when you talk about it?"

"Well, along with reconciliation, it helps to rid us from our sins. But the amazing thing about holy Communion, which is the real body and blood of Jesus, is not only how it unites us with Christ, but how it unites us with one another. The same sacrifice of the Mass that's going on now in Texas is going on in Africa and France and all over the world. With all the different kinds of people in the Church, it is the Eucharist that makes us one body," Danny said.

"I guess you could say that, because we all follow the same doctrine, there is a unity in our diversity."

"That's right," Danny agreed. "Tom, you mentioned the *Catechism*. That's a great tool we have now to spread our faith, to talk about the importance of the Eucharist and other doctrines. I think in the past a lot of people, including some priests, went through the motions celebrating the Mass. But the *Catechism* is so powerful and makes these doctrines so clear. I think that anyone who reads it with an open mind won't go through the motions anymore."

Although Danny's fiery rhetoric does not initially appear to strike a chord for Christian unity, he is correct in asserting that Catholics must know and rally around

Catholic doctrine if their dialogues with other faith traditions are to bear fruit.

"Are you developing any written materials for this foundation you're now working for?" I asked him.

"Well, I am working on a spiritual fitness workout guide," Danny offered. "In it, the believers are all part of one big football team, in which God the Father is the owner, and Jesus Christ is the coach."

I thought for a second, but I couldn't come up with a place for the Third Person of the Blessed Trinity on this team, so I asked Danny, who was now becoming a little distracted.

"What about the Holy Spirit?" I wondered.

"Oh, He's the personal trainer," Danny revealed. "Hey, Claudia and I need to be leaving for Mass now. Do you think you have enough?"

"Yes, it should be fine," I reassured him. "Pray for me at Mass, okay?"

Danny agreed, and then he was gone—gone to receive our Savior once again. And as he left, I knew that for someone making the transition from football player and coach to evangelist and prophet, Daniel Abramowicz was headed to the right place.

7. Mike Ditka

An "Iron Mike" with a Golden Heart

"So I tell you, her many sins have been forgiven; hence she has shown great love."

—Luke 7:47

He's a man of his word. Athletes as a group have a habit of making commitments and then breaking them, but if Mike says he's gonna do something, he'll do it.

—Fr. John Smyth on Mike Ditka

I was holding on the telephone line for Mike Ditka. But, unlike so many of the calls you make in this business, this one was different; I was not talking to some public relations person but to Diana Ditka, Mike's wife. And from what I could hear, Diana appeared to be relaying my message to the man himself.

"It's the guy who's writing that Catholic sports book again!" I could hear Diana explaining to her husband in the background. I could not decipher Coach Ditka's response, but one can guess the gist of it from Diana's answer. "I don't know," she told Mike. "I think Danny gave it to him" ("it" being the Ditka's home phone number).

Apparently this pleased Ditka enough to take the phone himself.

"This is Mike."

"Hello, Coach Ditka," I replied, quickly going into my spiel about the book and setting up a time to talk.

"Are you in New Orleans?" Mike asked, trying to pin me down.

"No, I'm actually in Chicago, Coach."

"Well, I'll be in Chicago tomorrow. Come down to my restaurant and we can talk."

"Chicago . . . tomorrow? That would be great!"

It was almost too good to be true. Not only was the interview happening and happening quickly—almost too quickly when you are used to these things taking months to transpire—but I was going to talk to Ditka in person. Certainly a live interview is always preferred to a phone chat, but it seemed almost *essential* in trying to capture the character of Ditka, who is perhaps the very definition of "larger than life."

Few sports figures have been both adored and abhorred as much as Mike Ditka, but few who knew him growing up in Aliquippa, Pennsylvania, would have predicted his football (let alone media) success. Just as Ditka's house did not stand out from any of the other row houses in the government subsidized condominiums called "the projects," neither did Mike stand out from any of the other throngs of kids that trounced in and out of them. As Mike said, "In our neighborhood, I was never the ringleader, just one of the guys." In fact, there was only one thing Mike seemed to excel in as a youth. Although all of his buddies participated in the usual juvenile pranks such as throwing tomatoes at houses or turning over garbage cans, "I was always the one who got caught," Ditka said. "And then when I'd go home, my dad would always whip my butt."

The results were no better for Mike on the football field, at least at first. Despite the fact that he loved football and played sports every day while growing up, as a 135-pound high school sophomore, Mike played sparingly in games, serving, instead, on the "hamburger squad" that scrimmaged against the varsity. "I got my butt whipped playing junior varsity that year," Ditka recalled, and while this whipping probably didn't damage him physically as much as when his dad literally took an old Marine Corps belt to his hide, it hurt his pride enough that he told his coach he was ready to quit.

Fortunately, Mike's coach, a man named Carl Aschman, was a rare individual who saw Mike's inner fire as well as his outward results. Aschman told Mike not only to keep playing, but that if he trained a little harder—and perhaps grew a little bigger—he would *start* the following year. Inspired, Mike began working out, doing sit-ups and push-ups so vigorously that the house shook. Next came calisthenics and cross-country, and when Mike finally got the growth spurt his coach had hoped for, he was ready. Mike started at linebacker his junior year, starring on a team that won the Western Pennsylvania League Championship. "Coach Aschman was a tremendous influence on my life," Mike summarized. "He could have agreed with the other coaches and said, 'Kid, you're too skinny and too slow to make it,' but he never did. He was the only one who always encouraged me, and that was so important in my not giving up. He wasn't just a good coach, but a tremendous person."

Both Mike's competitive and compassionate sides were on full display when my wife and I entered his restaurant and he ordered a somewhat shocked wait staff to seat us in a prime space usually reserved for those whose clothes cost more than I earn in a month.

"Want anything to drink?" Ditka asked us in a manner both polite and gruff, while at the same time shaking our hands. The Diet Cokes we ordered arrived almost as soon as the words left my mouth. So I began the interview by asking if it was true that his love for competition and sports came from his father and his love for God from his mom.

"Yeah, my dad was very competitive," Ditka said, while sipping on what appeared to be a 7-Up. It seemed fitting, when sizing up Mike in person, that he was a Bear most of his football life, because even at sixty, his height, broad shoulders, and muscular forearms made him resemble that animal more than any other. "Dad played semi-pro football until he got hurt, but he was competitive at everything he did. He was a welder in the steel mill and worked his way up to become president of the local union, and was a hell of a tough bargainer. But he also told me, 'The mill is not for you,' and that my opportunity to get out would come through sports."

"Was your dad religious?"

"No, he wasn't religious in that he didn't practice his faith. I think he was Russian Orthodox, but I don't remember him going to his church much, and he didn't come to Mass with us much either. But he was a good man, and he did have faith. I think religion is what one practices and faith in Christ and God is what one lives."

"So your mom was Catholic and was also responsible for raising you all Catholic," I surmised.

"Yeah, Mom was a convert, and she became a really devout Catholic—as converts usually are," Mike added.

"Your mom went to Mass every Sunday and always took you and your two brothers and sisters with?"

"Yeah. She went every Sunday, sometimes even during the week. Now she goes every day. And the only time I didn't sit with her was when I was serving as an altar boy."

"I read that you were an altar boy all through high school."

"Yes, I really enjoyed it. I even served as an altar boy in college."

"Really? You were an altar boy at Pitt?"

"No. But I would come back and serve when I was home," Ditka recalled.

"I also read that you wanted to go to Notre Dame over the University of Pittsburgh when you were in high school."

"I sure did," Ditka confirmed. "I always listened to Notre Dame on the radio, and back then just about every Catholic boy thought playing football at Notre Dame would be a great thing. And I got a recruiting letter from Jim Finks [then an assistant coach at Notre Dame, but who later gained fame as a Bears front-office man during the Ditka era], but then Jim took a job in Canada and I didn't hear from Notre Dame again for a long time, and by then I had decided on Pitt."

Pittsburgh's teams may not have been stellar during Ditka's years there—in fact, college was the only level of football at which Mike did not win a championship—but Ditka was, starring in three sports while there. Admittedly, Mike played basketball just like he played football. He once had Coach Adolph Rupp and a crowd of seventeen thousand Wildcat fans cussing at him after he knocked a University of Kentucky player into the third row on a pick, and Wisconsin coach John Erickson scolded, "You play like a bowling ball. You go out and knock all my players over!" But it was in football where the three-position (offensive end, defensive tackle, and punter) player earned All-American honors as well as the nickname "the Hammer." The Associated Press College Lineman of the Year was drafted #1 by both the Bears (in the National Football League) and the Houston Oilers (of the new American Football League). And although the Oilers offered him a good deal more money than George Halas's $12,000 (plus a $6,000 signing bonus), Mike wanted to play against the best—and he longed to be a Bear. So he turned down Houston and signed with Chicago.

Ditka's statistics in his first four years in Chicago compare favorably to those of any tight end in the history of football. In fact, Ditka was credited by many as making the tight end position into what it is today—transforming it from a blocking back who occasionally catches a pass to a vital pass receiving threat in the offense. Ditka caught 56 passes for 1,076 yards while being named NFL Rookie of the Year in 1961 and followed it with seasons of 58 in '62 and 59 during the Bear championship season in '63, a year that included many amazing runs, including the touchdown catch in which Ditka bounced off or ran over all eleven Pittsburgh Steelers, a run voted by the NFL as the greatest tight end play of all time.

In 1964, Ditka caught a career-high 75 passes with a dislocated shoulder and his arm in a harness most of the season, but by the following year, the injuries finally started to take their toll on his performance. Playing on a foot that was partially crushed in pre-season and never properly set (and thus never healed correctly), Ditka caught only 36 passes in 1965 and 32 in 1966. By the time his last year as a Bear rolled around, Mike, perhaps regretting he didn't take some of the big money the AFL offered, began to resent "Papa Bear" Halas and the relatively meager salaries he had received in Chicago. On the banquet circuit that winter, Ditka made the classic remark that Halas threw nickels around like manhole covers, and the relationship between the two soured, culminating in Ditka's being traded to the Eagles following the '66 season.

"Was George Halas at all religious? Did he ever lead the Bears in prayer before the games?" I wondered.

"No, he never did," Ditka confirmed. "It was one of the few teams that I played on that didn't pray," Ditka said, noting that his team prayed before the games at the University of Pittsburgh, and later with the Dallas Cowboys, and that he led prayers as head coach of the Bears and Saints. "I still prayed on my own before the games, but Halas never led us. But Halas was a good man and did a lot for players that people didn't know about."

In fact, Ditka was a lot like Halas, especially back then. While Halas was among the lowest paying owners in the league, "Papa Bear" also helped many of his players manage and invest their money. For example, Halas enabled Ditka to borrow $12,000 at very low interest with the help of his banker friends when Mike wanted to invest in a bowling alley, and financially helped Willie Galimore's and Brian Piccolo's families after each player died in his Bear prime (Galimore in a car accident in 1964, Piccolo of cancer a couple of years later). But as Ditka's career began to fade, Mike could have used someone to inspire him in— or help him understand—his faith, and Halas was not that person.

"It was important that I went through what I did in Philadelphia," Ditka said as one of Iron Mike's wait staff whispered something in his ear. "Philadelphia taught me humility," he said, looking me in the eye.

"It was crazy. We had just bought a house in Chicago, and here I was moving away from my family and friends. Life just wasn't fun anymore," he sighed.

At first, Ditka tried to look at the trade as a positive, a new opportunity. Despite the bad foot, Mike as well as the Eagles were respectable in 1967 as he caught 26 passes for the 6-7-1 team. But being away from his wife and kids during the season began to take its toll and, in 1968, Mike hit an all-time low.

In the first exhibition game, the Eagles played the Lions, and Franklin Field in Philadelphia was like concrete from the hot summer. Ditka tore a ligament in his heel that afternoon and neither Mike nor the team fully recovered. The Eagles started terribly that season (eventually losing their first eleven games), and Mike started drinking heavily. Separated from his family, not playing much (he caught only 13 passes for 111 yards that season), and feeling very alone, Mike went out partying every night, sometimes ending up back in his apartment, sometimes waking up with no idea where he was or how he got there. "Drinking hurt me physically *and* mentally. It made me lose confidence, and I lost confidence because I had no self-respect. I was trying to kill myself with the drinking."

"So you had about given up on yourself and your abilities . . . had you also given up on God?" I asked.

"No. As bad as I felt, I still prayed and went to Mass every Sunday. I didn't understand my faith that well, but I didn't give up on it," he said somberly.

Although this answer echoes perfectly with the one Abramowicz gives about his faith life during his Bourbon Street heyday, it must be hard for anyone never in that suicidal situation to understand. As for Ditka, he would (re)discover this person Jesus at his next stop in Dallas, and one of the men who would make Christ real again for him was his new coach, a man named Tom Landry.

At first Ditka—who had seriously pondered retirement after Philadelphia—didn't give a damn what happened to him in Dallas either. But he slowly began to admire the conviction of this coach who had taken a chance on him, and when he finally decided he wanted to play for Landry, Mike rededicated himself and gave it his best shot. Mike took advantage of the then-unique off-season training program the Cowboys offered, and got into the best shape of his life. And his hard work was rewarded, as he became an integral part of the Dallas offense during their Super Bowl seasons of '70 and '71. But despite his willingness to work and his desire to compete, multiple injuries stemming from his faulty foot finally forced Mike to retire in 1972, still without a sense of peace. Fortunately, Landry asked Ditka to stay on at Dallas as a coach, and Mike finally realized that there was something more important going on with his mentor than even winning.

Unfortunately, more hard times came to Mike before he started to see the light. During his last year as a player,

Mike separated from his first wife, Margie, and eventually obtained a divorce.

"Did you try to work things out?" I asked.

"Sure we did. We even got back together for a while when I was coaching at Dallas, but at our level of maturity then, it just didn't happen."

"You wrote in your autobiography that it was ninety-nine percent your fault."

"I wasn't around a lot—but that's a cop-out. I was just too stubborn to see the other side of things back then. But she's still my friend, the mother of my children."

"I also read that you rediscovered God when you started going to Bible studies as a coach in Dallas."

"Yes. I had a good Catholic upbringing, but I just didn't have an understanding of what those things meant. I had a job doing what I loved doing, was making good money, driving a nice car, but I was unhappy and I couldn't figure out why. Then I started to understand Scripture, to see that Jesus is the Way and the Truth and the Life, and I finally started to understand what happiness was."

"Weren't most of the players and coaches at the Bible studies evangelical Protestants?"

"Yes."

"Did you ever get the Catholic perspective during these Bible studies, perhaps from Roger Staubach?"

"Yeah, Staubach gave a Catholic perspective," Ditka said, slightly agitated. "But sometimes you don't need a Catholic to show you the faith. Remember the story of the Good Samaritan. Only one guy stopped to help that man on the side of the road, and he wasn't even a believer."

The famous Ditka temper was beginning to flare, but at the same time, I could see that it was the passion of his conviction—his belief that the Bible is the inspired word of God—that motivated his outburst. He said his understanding of Scripture was helping him share himself and be more patient. His new peace and understanding helped him not only to get to know Diana, whom he married in 1977 (and who is still at his side today), but to make peace with the "old man," George Halas, who in turn brought Ditka back as his head coach in 1982. Halas did not live to see his choice coach the greatest Bear team of all time, but Mike believes Halas saw it all in heaven, just the same.

"Coach, I notice a lot of the Catholic personalities I've interviewed for this book, from Holtz to Granato to Salazar, called winning a championship a 'miracle.' You, too, at one point, referred to the 1985 Super Bowl Bear team as 'miraculous.' In what sense would you call it a miracle?"

"What I thought was miraculous was how we went from being a team of individuals to becoming a family. There were a lot of barriers, a lot of obstacles to overcome, but we overcame them all and through it grew very close. The other thing about that team that was amazing is not only that they achieved the ultimate goal but had so much fun doing it."

"On the other hand many in the press criticized you in later years for winning only *one* Super Bowl with all the talent you had."

"I can't worry about what the press says!" Ditka snarled. "Tom, you wouldn't believe how many things that are written about me that are grossly untrue."

"Does it still bother you when you read those columnists whose comments are so personal that they go beyond game critiques and become outright character assassinations?"

"You try not to let it bother you, but sometimes it still does," Ditka admitted. "Deep down, everybody wants to be liked. And when some writer who passes himself off as your buddy writes a column of outrageous lies, it's hard."

"Well, don't feel bad," I told Mike. "The same thing happened to Lou Holtz when he was at Notre Dame. His situation was a lot like yours with the Bears. For both of you, it was your dream place to be a head coach; you were both there eleven seasons, and you each won one title. But although both of you turned the programs around, the press often criticized you for not winning *more* titles, as well as putting your own star above the teams. But in college, as you know, your team has to be voted number one, and after the '93 season, when it clearly looked like the Irish earned the top spot, beating the number-one Florida State Seminoles, the writers voted it to Florida State and the more popular Bobby Bowden. Can you imagine you trying to win the title if the writers voted on it?"

Ditka laughed. "Well, if I were voting, I'd give it to the number-one team, whether I liked the coach or not. But I could see where it'd be tough for me in that situation, too."

"I suppose the comparison doesn't end there," I continued. "After taking a couple of seasons off, Lou took the head job at South Carolina, and went 0-11. You had a few years in between the Bears' job and New Orleans . . . and things . . . well . . . probably didn't exactly end up like you had hoped for either."

Although I tried to phrase the transition gently, the memory still hit Ditka hard. "If you had paid *attention* to what I had said when I came to New Orleans, you wouldn't ask that! I said when I got there that God brought me to New Orleans for a reason. I was either going to get humbled or I was going to get exalted. As it turned out, I was, for the most part, humbled. It was tough, and the last year especially was not a lot of fun. But I still stand by what I said, and I don't regret my decision to coach again. I met a lot of good people in New Orleans, and that's the positive I'll take with me."

"So that would be one of the main reasons God had you there—because He had people there He wanted you to meet," I noted.

"I'm sure that's true," Ditka agreed.

"Was Danny one of the main people you got to know better?"

"Yes. Danny and his wife, Claudia, are very close to Diana and myself now."

"How about Ricky Williams?" I asked, recalling Ditka's lone pick in the 1999 draft, when Ditka not only traded away eight draft picks, but also donned a dreadlock wig in a famous *Sports Illustrated* photo to look like the prized prospect.

"Ricky right now is someone . . . who will not let a lot of people get close to him," Mike lamented. "But I liked Ricky Williams a lot. He had a tough season, too, with all the injuries, and I think in time he will open up more."

"As far as your faith goes . . . you said God brought you to Dallas so Landry could help you understand the importance of a personal relationship with Christ. Do you think God brought you to New Orleans so that Danny Abramowicz could help you understand Catholicism and the Catholic Church?"

"Landry helped, but a lot of people helped me in Dallas with my faith and many people helped me in New Orleans, too."

"But was Danny the main one in New Orleans? He's certainly inspiring when he talks about daily Mass, confession, the new Catholic Catholicism."

"You know, Danny has his faults, too!" Ditka snapped before quickly catching himself. "But if you need an on-fire evangelical Catholic to speak out about the faith, Danny's definitely your man."

"I guess the press is hard to deal with on the faith issue because they tend to concentrate on your faults, but the public accepts you because they see the goodness underneath . . . not to mention the tremendous amount of charity work you do."

"I never said I was perfect," Ditka stated. "God makes us the way we are, and we are supposed to glorify Him in everything we do. But sometimes our imperfections get in the way, and we have to ask His forgiveness . . . and I try to do that. As far as the charity work, I don't talk about my time at Miseracordia [a campus near Chicago for kids with special needs] or Maryville much because to me it's not a matter of whether anyone knows I do it or not. I'm not there because I want others to think I'm a good guy. I'm there because I enjoy being with the kids. I've *learned* a lot about life from being with them."

"What have you learned?" I wondered.

"Well, I've learned a lot about love. With most people in the world, the attitude is 'I will love you if you love me back.' But with these kids, love is unconditional. They love you whether you are a success or a failure, beautiful or ugly. It's like the good Lord said, 'Unless you become like little children . . .'"

"Because of your deeper understanding of the faith, the time you spend with and working with kids, has your attitude toward other people changed?"

"I really try to live by the Golden Rule now," Ditka said. "When I was young, I used to be very judgmental. If you dressed poorly or looked a certain way, I didn't like you or think highly of you. I don't think that way anymore."

"Are you looking forward to your new job [pre-game commentator] at CBS?" I asked.

"Yes, I am. It should be fun, and is a great way to stay involved in a game I truly love without the everyday pressure of coaching. I just hope I can justify CBS's faith in me."

Of course, there is little chance for failure here. Ditka has been one of the country's premier pitchmen since the Bears' "Super Bowl Shuffle" days, and his confident yet humble persona was so effective in the recent commercial he did for a financial planning firm that featured retired athletes, that many critics raved about his performance despite the fact he didn't say a word.

"Commercials? They are a good way to help yourself out financially, as well as keep myself in front of the public so people will watch me on CBS. As for that commercial [in which all that was needed from Ditka was his classic resigned expression], you notice I had a lot of lines."

"Tara Lipinski, who is also being featured in this book, was also in that commercial. Were you able to talk to her at all?"

"Yes. And, as a matter of fact, they originally had me holding the yarn that she was using to knit with, but they cut that scene out."

"Tara, as you know, has a very strong devotion to St. Thérèse."

"I like St. Thérèse a lot, too!" Ditka exclaimed.

"Are you especially devoted to any other saints?" I asked him.

"The Blessed Mother," Mike said emphatically. "I think that if you look at all the places that pay tribute to her— Lourdes, Fatima, and that one near Croatia—I can't pronounce the name."

"Medjugorje?"

"Yes. But all the places that pay tribute to her are special places, places where lots of miracles and conversions happen, so it's important to honor her. But I also think it's important to *not* talk just about being Catholic, because there are a lot of Christians out there who don't belong to the Catholic Church, and a lot of Catholics who go to church every Sunday but aren't very Christian."

Mike made good sense, but I felt I should counter with a return to the central experience of our Catholic worship, the Eucharist. Could it be, as several saints suggested, that many Catholics do not benefit much from the Sunday liturgy because they do not accept the Catholic teaching of transubstantiation?

"I believe that Jesus is really present in the Eucharist!" Mike asserted.

Reassured by his answer, my mind raced from Abramowicz's discussion of the Mass, to St. Augustine's teaching that the Eucharist was "our daily bread," to St. Pius X's famous statement that frequent reception of holy Communion was "the surest, easiest, shortest way to heaven." I wondered aloud if attendance at Mass during the week would help strengthen the "Sunday" Catholic.

"Sure, it would help," Ditka responded emphatically. "Why not go to the Eucharist more than once a week, to get regenerated?"

I then took the liberty of quoting Mother Teresa of Calcutta: "Receiving Jesus in the daily bread is how you get the strength to do good selflessly."

"Going to the sacraments is going to God," Mike agreed profoundly.

By this time, Mike was getting antsy, not because he wasn't interested in the topic, but because his staff were reminding him of another engagement, an on-camera endorsement he was to make for Bob Thomas, former Notre Dame and Bear place kicker now running for a seat on the Illinois Supreme Court.

Knowing my time was short, I said a short, silent prayer on how to close and ended up asking something I hadn't planned.

"Your wife, Diana, was very kind to me and a big help setting up the interview. But I couldn't find in any of the books or articles I read about you if she was Catholic, and I was wondering . . . "

"No," Mike confided. "Diana is a great person but grew up with no background in religion. She's always been a very kind, positive person who has done Christian acts without being raised a Christian."

"Like the Good Samaritan!" I chimed in. "Did she—or you both together—ever discuss the idea of her becoming Catholic?"

"We have," said Mike, pondering the question deeply. "I would really like her to get instruction in the faith . . . that is, when she is ready . . . Tom, they're calling me upstairs now. Do you think you've got enough?"

"Yes Coach, I sure do. Thanks."

"Before you go, could I get another picture of you," Jeanette asked, "standing next to Tom?"

"Sure. Hey, Tom, you stand on this step and I'll stand down here. That way you'll be as tall as me!" said Mike playfully.

The picture was soon snapped but the good-natured gesture was not forgotten. In a way, it was a silly thing to do, because it was quite obvious to anyone who knew us that not only am I not as tall as Mike, but that I will never stand as tall as he in the realm of wealth and worldly fame no matter how many stairs of the journalism ladder I climb. And yet, symbolically, it was the perfect picture, for Mike is not only a man who realizes his own imperfections and tries to correct them, but strives to show everyone he meets, from street beggar to president, that they are equals in his eyes as well as the eyes of God. And when I saw the developed picture and noticed that my head is slightly above his, I knew that Mike's big-heartedness had planned that, too, for he truly tries to put the needs of others above his own—which, for someone so in the limelight, may be the greatest miracle of all.

8. Cammi and the Granatos

A Family That Plays Together and Prays Together

When I was my father's child,

    frail, yet the darling of my mother,

He taught me, and said to me,

    "Let your heart hold fast my words:

    keep my commandments that you may live!"

                —Proverbs 4:3–4

Be doers of the word and not hearers only, deluding yourselves.

                —James 1:22

"How is your book going?" asked Ray Kavanagh, executive director of the Chicagoland Sports Hall of Fame.

"Fine, Ray. But I could still use a few more women athletes," I confessed.

"Why not try Cammi Granato," he suggested. "She gave a rousing, inspiring speech when she was inducted into the Chicagoland Sports Hall of Fame. And I'm pretty sure she's Catholic."

"Cammi Granato! That's a great idea," I said, resolving to go to the library as soon as possible to research her life and verify that she is a Catholic. Once there, an article detailing her praying the rosary with family members during her brother (and professional hockey star) Tony's hospital stay quickly convinced me of her devotion, but almost equally appealing was the fact that, smack-dab in the middle of two winter Olympics, she'd probably have some time to be interviewed. "I asked Cammi and she'd love to talk to you," said her agent, Kent Hughes, who paused for a second while he looked up her cell phone number. "This is great!" I thought to myself while on hold. A relatively short paper trail from the USA Hockey Headquarters to the Los Angeles Kings (with whom Cammi did radio broadcasts for a year) had placed me on the verge of conversing with the greatest of female hockey players, and I figured the interview was imminent as Kent got back on the phone with her number. "Like I said, Tom, Cammi would love to do it, so don't get discouraged if you don't get through right away. She is a little hard to get a hold of."

I'll say! As it turned out, catching Cammi for conversation proved as difficult as stopping the great Wayne Gretsky approaching the goal. Granted, Granato and the United States' women's hockey team were about to embark on another round of world championships (in which the U.S. eventually lost to old nemesis Canada in the finals in overtime), but even after that, getting a chat with Cammi proved no walk in the park. Finally, after another month or so of missed opportunities, I ended up talking to Cammi twice—the first time when she called me from the airport terminal during a layover between flights.

"Make sure you tell me when your team's flight is ready to leave," I told Cammi. "I sure don't want you missing your plane on account of my questions."

"Don't worry, I will," Cammi assured me good-naturedly. "I'm just glad I finally have a few minutes for you."

Actually, being good natured has become second nature for Catherine Michelle Granato. Just as her first two given names were combined early on into a uniquely feminine yet hockey-appropriate nickname, Cammi started in on the Granato family game as a young girl and never looked back.

"What got you hooked on hockey as a kid instead of, say, a more traditional woman's sport?"

"Well, I knew it was part of the family," Cammi answered. "My dad was very much into hockey [Cammi's mom and dad's first date was a Blackhawk game] and my older brothers were all playing by the time I started."

"Yes, I know your older brothers all played, and that Robby and Donny went on to play college hockey, while Tony became a star in the National Hockey League. But as a girl, there must have been another reason to pursue it past the fact that your brothers all played it."

"Yeah, you're right," Cammi conceded. "Hockey is not an easy sport to pick up. Learning how to stop and start is not only difficult, but sometimes painful. There's definitely no forcing anyone to learn hockey. So, beyond the family thing . . . I guess it just fits my personality. I'm pretty high strung, and don't like to sit still for long—and hockey's great for someone who likes to keep moving."

"I bet that was the one part of Sunday Mass you didn't like as a kid—the sitting still part."

"I'll say, Tom. I *liked* going to Mass as a kid, but I still remember my dad saying to me almost every week on the car ride there, 'Cammi, please calm down when we get inside.' Dad would constantly tell me not to fidget, but it was just really hard for me to stay in one place for a long time."

"She was always in motion," her dad, Don Granato, explains. "She could spill a glass of milk from across the table."

So, finding a game that not only allowed her to be in perpetual motion but actually expected her to rattle things was essential to Cammi finding herself, or at least her place in the world of athletics. At age six, she is getting ready by 6 a.m. to find some ice time before school. At age seven, her family moves to Downers Grove, Illinois, and her older brothers, Tony, Robby, and Donny, turn their spacious new basement into a hockey rink and their younger sister into the designated goalie, firing at her pucks of Kleenex wrapped in masking tape. Bloody lips and noses are her constant companion, but whenever her mom questions where they come from, she never implicates her siblings, knowing that if she does, she'll lose her spot in the not officially approved scrimmages.

At age eight, Cammi is not only playing on the local boys league, but is elected her team's captain, although she is then the only girl playing. "It didn't seem unnatural to me," said Cammi. "At that age, the [girls' and boys'] body types are about the same so there was no real physical difference." Of course, slowly but inevitably, these changes come, as do the attitudes that accompany them.

By the time she is in junior high, Cammi, still the only girl player, begins to get checked more, more than other players—which she doesn't mind as long as she knows it is coming. When a teammate hears an opposing coach telling his team Cammi's number and exhorting them to "get that girl," he tells Cammi, who switches jerseys with her muscular six-foot cousin, Bobby, and they all get laughs watching the opposition run into the youthful brick wall. But in a later tournament, when a kid-goon deliberately launches himself into Cammi, smacking her against the boards and leaving her crumpled body with a concussion, things are no longer so funny.

By her freshman year in high school, Cammi's biggest supporters, her mom and dad, ask her to get out of organized hockey, and she reluctantly agrees.

"That was a difficult time for me," Cammi commented. "For a long time I went around thinking to myself, 'I can't believe I have to quit.'" To help herself forget, she plays soccer, softball, basketball, and even handball. She wants to get to the Olympics like her brother, Tony, who played in them in 1988, and handball was then one of the few women's sports available. But it just wasn't the same. Cammi was born to play hockey and she had to find a way back.

"Was the hockey thing on your mind all through high school?" I asked Cammi.

"There are a million other things going on in high school, so that helped. And even though I didn't play organized hockey, I never gave it up completely. But I still thought about it often."

"What did your parents do when you talked about your hockey dreams?"

"My parents were wonderful. They always took the time to listen to me and encourage me, to keep hoping in my dream, even when it seemed impossible. 'You gotta have faith that these things will work out,' my mom [Natalie] always said—and I believed her."

"Did you even know there were a few colleges out East that had women's hockey teams?" I asked.

"I think it was my sophomore year in high school that I heard Providence had a team, and as soon as I found out, going to college there became one of my goals. But *how* that happened was really pretty lucky."

"Weren't you noticed playing in a tournament out East?" I inquired.

"Yes, but that in itself was pretty wild. I was actually scheduled to play in a women's soccer game that weekend, but some friends of mine told me about this hockey tournament which actually included a few girls, so at the last minute, I decided to enter. And as it turned out, John Marchetti [then coach of the Providence women's team] saw me playing and asked me to come. I can honestly say that if I didn't attend that one tournament, my life would have been far different."

So just like former Providence Friar Lenny Wilkens, who got a scholarship to the school largely on the basis of a most-valuable-player performance in one summer tournament, Cammi, too, gets accepted into the school, but not without some difficulty. "Actually, I didn't take all the right courses in high school I needed to get into Providence," Cammi recalls. "I needed to work out the [foreign] language requirement, and didn't finally get accepted until July."

But accepted she was, and when she debuted for the Lady Friars later that year, it marked the first hockey game Cammi ever played in with *all* women. Cammi recorded a hat trick (three goals) in that initial contest and went on to score 24 goals and make 22 assists that year to be named the Eastern College Athletic Conference Rookie of the Year. Subsequent seasons saw her progress to 48 goals, 32 assists and 41 goals, 43 assists. She also won three league MVP awards (while leading the Friars to two Eastern College Athletic Conference Championships) but, upon graduation from Providence, she was left feeling hungrier than ever for competition.

Cammi kept praying, and the Lord kept her playing. In her sophomore year, Cammi was picked for the U.S. National team in the first ever international women's competition; while in her junior year, the Olympic committee decided that women's hockey would indeed become an Olympic sport—but not until 1998, or six years in the future. Knowing she could not pass up that opportunity (but also realizing she needed to play more hockey in the meantime), Cammi decided after her senior season at Providence to enroll at Concordia College in Montreal to earn a graduate degree in sports administration—and play hockey against the best women Canada had to offer.

"It's kind of neat that every time your hockey career was about to end, a new opportunity arrived that enabled you to keep on playing."

"It sure is," Cammi agreed. "Sometimes I just look around and wonder, 'Where did all this come from?' Or I ask God 'Why am I blessed with all the good luck?' Someone once asked me if I felt cheated that there wasn't a women's professional hockey league to play in, but I said 'No! This is my dream!' Everything worked perfectly for me, whereas if I had been born even five years earlier, none of this competition would have been in place. So I'm just enjoying it, thankful each time God allows me another opportunity to keep playing."

"And Concordia was a positive experience for you, too?" I asked the school's three-time MVP and two-time Female Athlete of the Year.

"Yes. Each stop was not only positive but necessary for my development as a hockey player. At Providence, I learned the differences in the women's game as well as offensive strategy, whereas at Concordia, I learned how to play defense. Of course, we scored so many goals at Providence, I didn't have to play defense there!" Cammi laughed, but then paused to listen to someone else. "Tom, they're telling me I gotta go catch our plane now. Thanks for being patient. I'll talk to you soon."

"Soon" was probably not the most accurate word in retrospect, but after a month of nonfunctioning cell phones and last-minute cancellations, the interview resumed.

"Sorry about my cell phone," Cammi apologized, when she realized her faulty phone was not allowing me to get through. "You know we do get stipends from the United States Olympic Committee, but they are not much. A lot of times you are faced with a decision like, 'I'm gonna buy myself a new phone' or 'I'm gonna pay my rent.'"

Indeed, Cammi may have been "blessed with all the good luck" to have the opportunity to play hockey, but that did not make the going always smooth, or the defeats any easier. Six times, Cammi's United States team faced Canada in the championship game of the international competitions with a chance for gold, and each time, the Canadians sent the Americans home with silver. And each time she stood second on the awards podium, Cammi's face, according to her mother, became more and more "disgusted."

"I suppose you were a little sick of 'O Canada' by then," I said.

"Well . . . nothing against their national anthem . . . but *yes*!" Cammi admitted.

"But seriously, Cammi, did you ever start to think, after the fourth or fifth or sixth defeat, that although God gave you a great opportunity to play the game you loved for so long, that perhaps playing second fiddle to Canada was all there was, and it was time for you to say 'thanks' and go on to something else?"

"No, I *never* really thought that," said Cammi. "Of course in the beginning, we were overmatched against Canada and probably didn't stand a chance, but in the later years, we had the talent—we just had to figure out a way to win. I vividly remember standing at the blue line after that sixth defeat to Canada, asking some of my teammates what it would take for us to win next time, and we all resolved to go home and analyze why we kept coming up short. And the reason most of the players mentioned was that, although we worked hard whenever we were together on the ice, we had to grow closer off the ice in order to succeed."

"Becoming friends outside of practice would help you become a better team once the game started?"

"Yes," she said.

"Well, you can't argue with success," I noted. "But before we get into Olympic glory, we should probably talk about the one event that more than any of the defeats, made you wonder if hockey was such a good thing after all."

"You mean . . . Tony's injury?"

"Yes."

Cammi's brother, Tony, had been in the National Hockey League for eight years and was an established star when he took a vicious check from Hartford Whaler Rob Brown on January 25, 1996. Tony began complaining of headaches after that game but still played two days later. However, not only did the headaches get worse, but Tony started having trouble remembering names. Tests showed bleeding on the brain and, on February 16, the doctors performed a four-hour brain surgery to remove the damaged blood vessels. Although the surgery was not only potentially career-ending but life-threatening, Tony pulled through with no ill effects. In fact, not only did he experience no memory loss or slurred speech, but he returned to hockey and played well enough to be named to the NHL all-star game the next season. Still, it was pretty tough for Tony and his family as it transpired.

"Now, it's easy for me to look back and say I'm stronger for the experience," Cammi said. "But at the time, first hearing about the 'hit,' then about Tony's memory loss, and then his need for brain surgery . . . at first I was mad. I was asking God 'Why?' I couldn't understand how a game I loved—*we* loved—could be threatening to take my brother's life. I questioned my faith, but eventually my faith got me through it."

"I read that your family gathered around Tony before the surgery and said the rosary."

"Yes. Before they took Tony down [to surgery], my family all joined hands and took turns saying the prayers. During the surgery, I turned to God more than at any other time in my life. It was scary—you're just waiting to see if he's okay, but at the same time, someone could walk up to you and tell you he isn't."

"In the end then, the ordeal strengthened your faith," I said.

"Yes. It was a great growing experience," Cammi explained. "Before that, I used to think that hockey was the greatest thing in life, but this made me realize that, as positive a thing that hockey is, it's not the most important thing. God is."

"Do you think incidents like Tony's point out the flaws of NHL hockey, not only the excess, extra-curricular checking, but the World Wrestling Federation-type fights that league officials continue to allow?"

"Yes, I do. I know some fans come to see the fights, but I believe that stuff really cheapens the game. As for checking, I agree with you that the checking that occurs away from the puck could be eliminated. In the women's game, most refs allow a certain amount of incidental checking when two players are going for the puck, but that's it. And because of it, the women's game seems to create a much more wholesome viewing environment for the family."

Speaking of the family (besides her three hockey brothers, Cammi is also cheered by older sister, Natalie, and younger brother, Joey), the Olympic games were certainly a family affair for the Granatos. Cammi's father and mother and siblings were there, most attending their second Olympics, having watched Tony play for the U.S.A. ten years earlier. Her dad, Don, gave Cammi a "love" letter before the first game, while Cammi simultaneously wrote one to her parents about how much she loved them and her brothers and sister, and how much they had contributed to her success.

"Did you know your dad had written you a letter when you wrote yours?"

"No—it was a surprise. But I guess since Tony's surgery, we've all learned to tell each other important things right away and not wait."

"Not only did you two write each other touching letters without the other knowing about it, I read that your brother Robby also wrote you, only his was in the form of a poem."

"Yes. I still use it. It was called *Turning Silver into Gold.* It talked about how I had spent all of my life preparing for this and now I should seize the moment, play as hard as I could, and when it gets tough and you need a little extra push, we [the family] would provide it!"

"As it turns out, you probably did need a little extra push," I said. "Going into the games you had a back injury, were suffering from anemia, and thus not nearly at full strength."

"I never wanted to look at it like that," Cammi stated. "True, I couldn't do strength training because of my back, and I found out after the games that I was protein deficient, but I never felt sick. I was in good cardio-vascular shape, and I was peaking mentally. Spiritually I was strong. I was just so happy to have this chance, I just looked at the back injury as another challenge."

United States team captain Cammi scored the first goal in women's Olympic history and remained the inspirational leader of the squad as they marched their way into the finals against none other than their old nemesis, Canada, the team that had always beaten them. Of course, the team would turn to Cammi one more time, and she would turn to God.

"I'm sure you pray before every game, but did you pray any differently before the gold medal encounter?"

"Yes. Normally I pray for strength that I play my game, that I have my legs . . . but I remember sitting in bed the night before, realizing how much the one game could change my life."

"In what way?"

"Well, I knew if we won the gold, it would not only validate us as a team, but bring me a lot more opportunities to talk, to promote women's hockey, my faith, even endorse products—and I got to thinking there's a very fine line in winning, and how difficult it is to weigh all the good and the bad that comes with it . . . So as much as I wanted to win, I just thanked God for leading me to this point, for giving me the joy to compete and blessing me with the opportunity to achieve all that I have already achieved—and again just asked Him to allow me and my team to play our best, and I left the outcome in His hands."

Well, Cammi's dream, her brother's poem, and the hopes of American hockey fans all came true that next day, as the United States beat Canada 3-1 to take home the gold, and Cammi's story was so inspiring that the team captains of all the other United States teams voted that Granato should carry the American flag in the closing ceremonies. "To be chosen by all our captains to carry our flag . . . I was so excited. Really, Tom, there was no bigger honor for me *ever* than that!"

Two years later, the glitter and glamour of being an Olympic hero has died down, but the good Cammi accomplishes because of her achievement has not. With her family, she founded the Golden Dreams for Children Foundation and raised $100,000 in its first year for the Ronald McDonald Children's Hospital of the Loyola Medical Center in Maywood, Illinois (the hospital where Cammi was born). "Last year we raised the money to help children with asthma," Cammi explained. "But this year, I think we're going to try a new thing, an educational program—that will help kids learn to respect each other, to show healthy kids what it is to walk in the shoes of a classmate or teammate who suffers from a disability."

"That's a great idea," I told her. "Has your prayer life also changed since the Olympics?"

"I still pray when I'm worried or afraid. I also pray to know the right thing to do."

"Do you pray any particular prayers?"

"I pray the Our Father. My parents taught me that when I was young, and I still say it often."

"Do you say any special novenas, or have any devotions to particular saints?"

"I don't . . . I mean, you can pray all the time and go to church as much as you want, but you have to practice what you believe in your daily life. *That's* what I see lacking in society! Human respect!"

"Well . . . I bet you're at least able to sit still at Mass now, right?"

Cammi laughed. "I'm *better* at it. But I guess that is one thing I really like about the Catholic faith. It not only teaches respect for human life, but does something about it."

Obviously, on the active versus contemplative scale of Catholicism, Cammi is still more of the former, but as she was still single, I wondered if she had considered all of her vocational options.

"I know you had a boyfriend for a long time . . . but right now you're not really . . . well, engaged or anything, so I was wondering if you ever thought about, well . . . "

"I think I know where you're going with this one. Yes, I do want to get married someday!"

"Have you ever thought about becoming a nun?"

"No, I mean it's not for me. I've always wanted to have a big family. I wanted a bunch of kids, six or seven at least, but obviously, at twenty-nine, I might have to revise that number down a little bit."

While at the present time Cammi certainly plans on playing in the 2002 Olympics in Salt Lake City, she hinted her desire to start a family might take precedence—given the right guy of course.

"Tom, I still love hockey and I'd love to do both [have a family *and* continue competitive hockey], but I don't know if that's possible.

"Who knows, Cammi. Suzie McConnell-Serio never thought it would happen, and suddenly she's a starting point guard in the Women's National Basketball Association."

"That would be *great*," agreed Cammi, referring to her dream about a women's pro-hockey league, which was talked about in 1998 but never materialized. "As it is, Salt Lake City looks like the [logical] end of the line, but if that happened . . . "

"Well, your hockey luck has been pretty good so far!"

"Yes, it has," Cammi laughed. "But seriously, the older I get, the more I want to start a family, too. I love being an aunt [Cammi is a frequent babysitter for her brothers' children], and I can see from this view what a sacrifice being a parent is. It's a twenty-four-hour commitment; the biggest in your life . . . but it's also what I long for."

"Well, thanks again for your time, Cammi. It was great talking to you."

"Thank you, Tom. You've been more than patient!"

"Cammi, before you go, is there any one thing that you would say is the most crucial to your Catholic faith?"

Cammi did not take long to answer this one. "I guess that would be the care and love of my family. My faith tells me that they are always with me—even my grandparents, who are now in heaven—and they will always give me that extra help when I need it. I just don't know where I'd be without my family. Thanks again."

With that, Cammi hung up the phone to head back to that hockey highway, in search of a goal she hasn't yet reached—or scored as the case may be. But as God saw it fitting that Cammi's ice career continue when hope was dim, it seemed only right for a daughter so dedicated to her family that the Lord would soon provide the opportunity for her to start one of her own.

9. Coach Ray Meyer

Laughing with a Legend

In the evening of your life, you will be judged by how much you have loved.

—St. John of the Cross

"**H**e's at camp?" my wife exclaimed. "You mean Ray's still coaching?"

Yes. At eighty-six, Ray Meyer, All-Star player at Notre Dame and winner of 724 games during his forty-two years of coaching at DePaul, was still coaching. And why not? In a life where millions came to know him as "Coach"—while at the same time touching thousands personally in that capacity—you could hardly expect Ray to stop just because old age had slowed him down a step or two. That would have been like Mother Teresa taking a desk job.

"Yes, I'm still coaching," Ray confirmed when I tracked him down at his Wisconsin summer haven. "This is my fifty-second year of doing my summer camp, and even though it's not much of a moneymaker anymore, I still come."

"Why do you still do it?"

"I love the kids," Meyer confided. "I still go out onto the courts every day. I was just talking to Al McGuire [former Marquette coach, who passed away January 26, 2001], and he told me, 'Ray, you must be nuts! You should hire people to run the camp for you!' But Al knows I still enjoy it . . . and not just the coaching. I really enjoy being around the kids, doing things with 'em. Why, just the other day we were out on the lake, the kids were swimming and I was in this big inner tube, and we all started splashing one another."

Although there's no doubt that Ray's still a kid at heart, he was not exactly a meek type when he was growing up. The youngest of ten children, "Baby" Ray more than held his own in a tough Chicago west-side neighborhood that produced boxing greats Barney Ross and Davey Day. And while Ray was always a religious boy, he often mixed faith with fisticuffs, as the following story illustrates.

"My brother, Joe, and I, were walking to church one Sunday, dressed in our Sunday best, when we saw a man trying to crank-start his Model T. This guy couldn't get the thing going for anything," Ray recalled, "so when Joe offered to start it for fifty cents, he agreed. Well, Joe crank-started it, but he started it so quickly that the man said he was only going to pay us a quarter. Joe and I told him he had to stick to the original agreement, but he refused."

"So, then, what did you do?"

"We beat the devil out of him until he gave us the money," Ray replied, and then the Meyer boys proceeded on to Mass, with clothes and souls in less than immaculate condition.

In retrospect, Ray could hardly be blamed for his "tough faith." First of all, Meyer's dad died when Ray was only thirteen, so the family had to struggle for every dime (or quarter) they could get. Second, the priests of that era (and area) often encouraged such behavior.

"I was playing in a big game for St. Agatha's [his local parish team], and a fan on the Blessed Sacrament [the opposing school] side of the stands was riding me, calling me obscene names. Finally, Fr. Danny O'Rourke [a parish priest] came up to me and asked, 'Are you gonna let him get away with that?'

"Well, I figured I couldn't argue with a priest, so I went up into the stands and flattened the guy with one punch." As you might imagine, a riot that dwarfed the melee in John Wayne's *The Quiet Man* broke out, and the game was "postponed," with St. Agatha's winning the rescheduled match behind closed doors.

Yet, whether Ray came home with another sports-related injury or another stray dog (at one time the Meyer home had accumulated five such mutts), Ray's mom, Barbara, a regular at the weekly Our Lady of Sorrows Novena down the street, was there to welcome him home and encourage his Catholicism. In fact, Ray's faith became so evident that a priest convinced him to enroll in Quigley Preparatory Seminary, the local high school for boys studying for the priesthood. And Ray did find his vocation there, but it was behind the bench, not the altar, where Meyer would leave his lifelong mark.

For even while at Quigley, Ray ended up spending as much time at the gym as in the church. Noticing his passion, old friend Fr. O'Rourke asked him to coach the St. Agatha's girls team, where a talented young Irish lass named Margaret Mary Delaney soon caught his eye. After one game, Ray got her attention by trying to shoot popcorn kernels into her soda, then asked her out. Both Ray and the kernels connected, as Meyer dropped out of Quigley and "Marge and Ray" eventually became husband and wife.

After graduating from St. Patrick's High School—and leading them to win a national Catholic high school basketball championship—Ray briefly attended Northwest-ern University before money problems sent him back home. Ray, thanks once again to Fr. O'Rourke's maneuvering, eventually ended up at Notre Dame on a basketball scholarship—but only after International Harvester, the company where Ray had been working, promised Ray's job to his brother, Joe Meyer, so that his mother was provided for.

At Notre Dame, Ray's love of our Lady grew, and his faith in God increased. Of course, much of faith is hard work, and as a freshman, Ray bagged peanuts for the varsity games, waited on tables at the dining hall, and borrowed his roommate's textbooks, because he couldn't afford to buy his own. Ray did eventually find time for basketball, leading Notre Dame to a 62-8-1 record (as well as two national championships) during his three years on the varsity. By his senior year, Ray not only was elected team captain, but had taken over the lucrative peanut concession at games, and won the 1938 Byron V. Kanaley Award for outstanding student-athlete, and more importantly the $125 stipend that went along with it. So armed with several hundred dollars and a sociology degree, Ray left Notre Dame a rich man—although it was neither the money (not a bad sum for a depression era lad) nor the diploma he earned there that gave him the most security.

"Notre Dame deepened my religious devotion," Ray related. "It was there that I first really learned how to pray." Of course, in those days, attendance at Mass was mandatory, and his coach required the team to say the rosary before every game, but Ray also went to the Grotto to pray each and every day during his four years there. "A lot of the guys made jokes about me praying all the time," Ray told me, "but something just drew me in, and I could rarely pass by the Grotto without saying at least a quick Hail Mary. I just felt that when I was there, her prayer did wonders."

Ray spent one "depressing" year as a social worker, recalling that "everyone was out of work then, and they needed more help than we could give." Thus, he decided to get back into basketball, coaching an Amateur Athletic Union team and refereeing Catholic Youth Organization games on the side. Finally, Ray got a job offer to teach and coach at Joliet High School—only to turn them down when they offered him one hundred dollars less a year than he had asked for! Ray left the interview second guessing himself, when that very night, he got a call from Notre Dame to be interim coach, as Irish head coach George Keogan had suffered a mild heart attack and Fr. Hugh O'Donnell wanted him to sit out the remainder of the year as a precaution. Meyer jumped at the chance and practically flew to South Bend, where he led the Irish to an 11-1 mark the rest of the way. Meyer then stayed on as Keogan's assistant for the 1941-42 season, but when the year ended, Ray got a job offer from a small Catholic college back in Chicago. Reluctant to leave the Golden Dome at first, Meyer let Keogan convince him to at least try his hand at being a head coach, and Ray finally headed to DePaul, where a meager three-year contract turned into a forty-two-year run. And as fate would have it, another shy young man, a man who also initially studied for the priesthood, would be the man who turned Meyer into a coach.

When George Mikan first arrived at DePaul, he had little natural talent and had already been turned down by many bigger universities, including Notre Dame. But George had heart—and did he have height! At 6'10", Mikan was then the second tallest player in the country—if only Meyer could teach him to play.

Meyer tried everything. To increase Mikan's foot speed, Ray made him jump rope. To aid his hand coordination, he had George box. To gain rhythm, he forced Mikan to take dancing lessons. And all this was off the court!

After each regular practice was over, Meyer had Mikan shoot two to three hundred hook shots with each hand. Then George would play one-on-one with speedy 5'4" guard Billy Donato to improve the center's lateral movement. "I was a slave driver, but he was a willing slave," Meyer recounted. "I was young and full of energy, and George wanted to be a great player."

And it all paid off, beyond both men's wildest dreams. Not only did Mikan lead DePaul to two National Invitational Tournament championships (then considered college's "National Champion"), but George was later voted by sportswriters as the greatest basketball player of the half century. Meanwhile, the Mikan experience convinced Meyer that he had found his calling. Ray now knew he would not be leaving coaching anytime soon.

Still, right from the start, Ray had to fight for the place of faith in athletics. "Before Mikan would shoot his free throws," Meyer mentioned, "he would always make the sign of the cross, which was very uncommon in those days. The opposing fans would give George a lot of flack about it, especially down South. Finally I went to Fr. O'Malley [DePaul president] and told him that Mikan was getting a lot of jeers when he made the sign of the cross before free throws and should I ask him to stop?

"'How has Mr. Mikan been doing this year on his free throws?' Father asked.

"'Quite well, Father,' I told him.

"'Then tell him to continue,' Father replied."

Other issues involving the faith were not solved quite so easily. When Ray began coaching, there were no black players at any of the major colleges. "During the war years, the Great Lakes Naval Academy team practiced at DePaul, and they had several tremendous black players. They'd sometimes ask me if they could enroll at DePaul once their military stint was up, and I'd tell them, 'If you guys were on the same team as Mikan, *nobody* would ever beat us. The problem is, no one would ever *play* us.'"

While a few coaches, like Kentucky's infamous Adolph Rupp, flat out told Meyer, "If you bring black players, we can't play you anymore," in reality there was a silent agreement among them not to bring blacks into their schools and onto their rosters. Finally, after Jackie Robinson broke the color line in baseball in 1947, a few blacks started to trickle in, but they were treated horribly, from racial epithets being yelled at them during games, to being turned down at restaurants and hotels the team stopped at. "If a restaurant told us our black players would only be served if they ate outside, I'd tell the owner the hell with it, we'll all eat outside. We ate a lot of meals at bus stops back then."

"Couldn't Catholic colleges just all get together and say we are going to recruit black players and if no one wants to play us, we'll just play each other until this thing is settled?"

"Because Catholic universities didn't *want* to play each other that often!" Ray interjected.

"I remember Knute Rockne once said he didn't want to schedule other Catholic schools because it divided the loyalties of Catholic fans who by then had pretty much gravitated toward Notre Dame."

"That was part of it, but part of it was financial. Every game was important, but games against other Catholic universities were life and death, for the outcome would often decide where many boosters/fans would send their contributions that year."

So while DePaul struggled to find its Catholic athletic identity, Ray, a Catholic husband and father of six, struggled to make ends meet. For a dozen years, Ray coached a team of college all-stars against the Harlem Globetrotters once the regular season was over, and then spent the rest of the summer in Wisconsin, coaching kids in his basketball camp. Now in its fifty-second year, the famous camp almost didn't survive its first.

"Father Charles Williams [a pre-med professor at DePaul] kept telling me that there was a great need for a Catholic summer boys camp, and that I was the perfect man to run it, and before I knew it, I had spent five thousand dollars for a plot of undeveloped woodland in northern Wisconsin. I spent all that first summer just chopping down trees with Ed Mikan [George's brother]. Finally, we had to get rid of all the brush, so we stuck it in the middle of an open field and tried to set it on fire, but it was too green. So we poured a ton of gasoline on it."

"Gasoline! I bet it lit up then."

"Did it ever! In fact, it went so high that sparks started to fly, and a large portion of the forest started on fire. People from the town came to try to put it out, but nothing seemed to work. Finally, I told Marge and the kids to go out on a boat in the lake, and I called Fr. Williams."

"Father Williams?"

"Yes. This thing was beyond our control, and he had gotten me into this mess."

"So, what did Father do?"

"He had us all kneel down by the fire and led us in a prayer. Within minutes, a cloud appeared directly over the fire and it started to rain. It rained hard enough and long enough to put that fire out . . . but the funny thing was, in the cabins less than a mile away, people told me it did not rain at all."

Back at DePaul, Meyer continued to enjoy moderate success, although nothing like the championship seasons of the Mikan era. One reason was the facilities; not only were there few dorms and virtually no campus, until 1956 the Blue Demons practiced in the "Old Barn"—along with every other athletic team at DePaul. Actually, the "Old Barn" was a converted theatre, and holding practice there was a virtual circus. "The boxing club would get the old stage," Meyer recalled, "while the track team got one-third of the floor and mostly ran hurdles. So we got the other two-thirds of the floor and practiced lengthwise, but we had to be careful because any high shots or passes would hit the skylights. On top of everything, we'd often have Michael O'Connell [then university president] sitting up in one of the old theatre boxes, chain smoking during our practices."

"Really?"

"Yeah. Father O'Connell loved to watch the boys practice—said it was good for his spirits."

"If not your players' lungs."

Meyer laughed. "Someone once said they'd like to make a movie of my life, but I wasn't interested at the time. But looking back, those practices in the Old Barn would have made a great scene."

And so, despite Meyer's expertise, DePaul's limited budget finally caught up with them. Then, in 1970-71, Ray suffered his worst season ever, finishing 8-17. Attendance had dropped to around a thousand a game, the athletic department had virtually cut out scholarships, and Ray, frustrated with the situation, was ready to retire. But with the help of some supporters, Ray presented his case for more scholarships and better equipment to DePaul chancellor, Cumberford O'Malley, and Fr. O'Malley decided to give the basketball program more money on a three-year trial basis. DePaul built athletic dormitories, and Ray not only hired a full-time assistant but also was awarded a part-time assistant—his son, Joey—to be solely in charge of recruiting. And recruit he did!

By bringing such stars as Mark Aguire, Terry Cummings, and Clyde Bradshaw to DePaul and the improved Chicago campus, Joey helped Ray experience the heyday of Blue Demon basketball during the twilight of his father's career. Ray went 180-30 in his last seven seasons with the Demons, including an incredible 79-6 record from '79-'80 to '81-'82 with a National Collegiate Athletic Association Final Four appearance, as well as a National Coach of the Year Award in 1979. Ray personally traces DePaul's rise to a 1978 nationally televised come-from-behind overtime victory against his alma mater, when Gary Garland sank a thirty-foot buzzer-beater to defeat Notre Dame 69-68.

"I got more mail after that game than after any other I coached," Ray told me. "And a lot of the letters were about their prayers."

"Prayers?"

"An old woman from California who knelt down in front of her TV set to pray for us when we were down by five in overtime; a pastor in Buffalo who said the tide turned when he put a statue of St. Vincent DePaul on top of the TV set."

"Do you think these prayers really helped?"

"I'd kid Digger Phelps [Notre Dame coach at that time] that whenever he went to an early morning Mass before our games to light a candle for Notre Dame, I'd always go to a later Mass and blow it out, and then relight it for DePaul. But seriously, prayer does give you confidence. If your opponents have much greater talent than you do, prayer is not going to make up the difference. But, if the talent of each team is equal, prayer makes you feel you can't lose."

And if there was one thing that separated Ray's career from that of the other Hall of Fame coaches, it was prayer. No matter where they were playing, Ray made sure he went to Mass the day of a game—which created some interesting scenarios. "In Stillwater, Oklahoma, we had to drive down to a Catholic grade school to find a priest who would say Mass for us—and then he invited the whole junior high to attend! Once we got in late to Terre Haute for a game against Indiana State, and when an attending priest found out I hadn't been to Mass yet, I sent the team out for warm-ups with the assistant coach, and he said Mass for me in the rest room. And there was the time we were waiting for a flight at O'Hare, and Joey found out I hadn't gotten to Mass yet, so he had the team chaplain say it for us in the middle of the airport. Although we didn't intend it at the time, it must have been quite a witness."

And, of course, there was the rosary. "The players used to call me 'the man with the beads,' as I was never without one. Before each game, I'd send the team out of the locker room, but I'd join them only after I said a few decades. Then right before tip-off, I'd gather the team around me and we'd say a Hail Mary—even in the late '70s when there were no Catholics among DePaul's starting five. Now . . . I say the rosary to ask my wife, Marge [who died in 1986] and my daughter Mariann [who died of cancer in 1996] to help me through each day." He paused, "It's tough now . . . tough without Marge. Even at camp . . . which I still love . . . there are more kids who get in trouble, but that's only because there are more kids from broken homes. But I still try."

Later, when Ray is back from camp and has invited Jeanette and me over to his house, Ray continues on with this same thought. He shows me the mounds of novenas he says every night. They are stacked on the coffee table in front of his big-screen TV—his current combination of faith with sports. "Did you read the article Rick Telander wrote about me?" Ray asks between the photos my wife takes. He was referring to a recent feature by the *Chicago Sun-Times* writer that talked about how Ray has visited his wife's grave every Saturday for the past fourteen years.

"Yes, yes, I did Coach. It was well written and very moving . . . I hope to do as good a job as Rick did, but hopefully I can show your Catholic faith better."

Then, at this point, I decided to share with Ray a story about how his life of faith serves to inspire faith in others. "Ray, you never know about some things. Not long ago, I was working at that liquor store down the street from you to help make ends meet. A young woman used to come in there every day to buy beer, and each day, it looked like she was going downhill a little bit more. But just when I thought this girl was hopeless, she came in one day bursting with excitement, like a young kid. When I asked her what she was so happy about, she said she had just bumped into Coach Ray Meyer down at the hardware store! And because of that one experience with you, I was able to start talking to her about her faith, and she began to cut back on her drinking and started to regain the hope she needed to take control of her life . . . all because of that one time she met you at Ace."

As I was talking, a tear started to form in the coach's eye, but it was quickly overcome by his legendary smile. "Of course, sometimes it happens the opposite way, too. Once I was the grand marshal of a parade and a lady ran up to me, put her arms around me and says, 'It's so nice to meet you, Mr. Halas!'"

"She thought you were George Halas?"

"Right. And when I said I wasn't, she started to apologize. 'I'm so sorry, Mr. Ditka.' So when I finally told her who I was, she said somewhat annoyed, 'Well, I knew you had to be *somebody* famous!'"

We laughed, the three of us. But as my wife and I were leaving, we realized that there was now more to it than just mere laughter. For in the evening of his life, Ray lived to make people laugh, but would die happy if they could only dream his dream.

10. Sammy Sosa

The Happy Slammer

*Rejoice in the Lord always. I shall say it again,
rejoice! Your kindness should be known to all.*

—Philippians 4:4

*. . . By hard work of that sort we must help the weak,
and keep in mind the words of the Lord Jesus who
said, "It is more blessed to give than to receive."*

—Acts of the Apostles 21:35

Tom,
I will leave you a media pass on Tuesday. The press gate opens at
3:35. I would suggest you arrive about 4 p.m., then approach
Sammy when he's not busy during batting practice . . . Sorry
this has taken so long . . . Benjie

"**T**hank God!" I thought as I read the e-mail realizing my
request (my dream) to meet the happy home-run man
himself was about to happen.

It had been almost a year since my initial media request
to talk to Sammy, and I'm sure I could write a book (*How
to Obtain an Interview with a Major Celebrity*) on this experience alone. There were so many ups and downs—the most
notable being when I was finally put on Sosa's schedule
and then Sammy (through his agent) demanded to be
traded and canceled all his interviews.

But I'm getting ahead of myself. I first want to offer a

brief overview of Sammy's career (and my pursuit of it)—
for without it, only those closest to Sammy could ever
comprehend why our brief conversation was so hard to
obtain, and why the wait was worth it.

Samuel Peralta Sosa was born in the Dominican
Republic town of San Pedro de Macoris on November 12,
1968, the fifth of seven children. His early years were relatively comfortable, but that all changed when Sammy was
five and his father, Juan Montero, died. Sammy and his
family were forced to move into a tiny two-bedroom
apartment, their mother, Mireya, was obliged to work full
time for a food delivery service, and Sosa and his siblings
entered the workforce. Sammy started as a shoe-shine boy,
and later "progressed" to selling oranges and washing
cars. Although Sammy did not know it at the time, one of
his car clients was George Bell, a Dominican baseball
player who was a young star in the major leagues. As fate
would have it, the next time their paths crossed, in 1992,
was when a young unproven White Sox outfielder (Sosa)
was traded to the Cubs for their established veteran (Bell).
But the real irony of the situation was that most scouts
then believed the Cubs got the worst end of the deal.

But despite the fact that the Dominican Republic had
long been a hotbed for baseball talent, with then-current
players Bell, Julio Franco, and Joaquin Andujar, and past
Dominican stars such as Juan Marichal and Rico Carty
(who was from Sammy's hometown), Sammy was too
busy working to be concerned about baseball, either with
hero worship or actual playing. When Sammy finally did
find a little time for leisure, he went into boxing—a sport
that his mother abhorred. Finally, at fourteen, Sammy not
only obeyed his mother and gave up fisticuffs, but he took
older brother Luis's advice and tried baseball for the first
time. Two years later, Texas Ranger scout Omar Minaya,
who in his report noted a 5'10", 150-pound kid who
"appeared to be malnourished . . . has a wild loopy swing

but a strong arm, good bat speed, and a real inner fire," signed Sosa to a minor league contract for the meager sum of $3,500. Elated, Sammy bought himself a bicycle, then went home and gave the rest of his money to his mother.

Sammy's progress as a young player was unsteady—something to be expected of a kid who not only started playing baseball late and was unschooled in the fundamentals, but of a teenager being transported to a land (Sammy came to the Rangers' Florida farm team shortly after signing) he did not know and a language he did not understand. In 1989, at the age of twenty-one, Sammy was still overthrowing the cutoff man and swinging at pitches in the dirt, but his raw talent was so tremendous that the Rangers gave the phenom a shot at the "show," the players' slang for the major leagues. Things looked bright at first, as Sammy had two hits in his first game, and found a mentor in veteran Ranger and fellow Dominican, Julio Franco.

But after a fast start, Sammy trailed off to a .238 average with only one home run and twenty strikeouts in 84 at bats—and was shipped back to the minors. There, the Rangers gave up on him and traded him to the White Sox—with whom Sammy had similar results. After another fast start (3 for 3 with a home run in his first White Sox game, then finishing the year hitting .273 in 33 games for Chicago), disappointment followed when Sammy hit .233 for the Sox in 1990, then .203 in 1991. As a result, he was again demoted to the minors and was again traded—this time to the Cubs.

The Cubs, though, were the first team to truly commit to Sammy, telling him he was their new everyday right fielder. After an injury-ridden 1992 season, Sosa rewarded the Cubs' faith in him by hitting 33 home runs and driving in 93 in 1993. Sammy's play was far from perfect, however: he committed nine outfield errors, and was still somewhat impatient at the plate, striking out 135 times compared to only 38 walks. But his rare combination of power and speed appeared to be the signs of a future superstar—or were they? Sammy became only the fourteenth major leaguer ever to enter the rare "30-30 club" (30 home runs and 30 stolen bases in the same season), but how he handled this accolade was a perfect example of how far Sammy had come as a player and a Christian—and how far he needed to go.

Sammy's generosity, which would become a trademark later in his career, was fully evident after his breakout season. Following his feat, Sammy first bought his mother a house and then donated one million dollars to his hometown of San Pedro de Macoris for the building of the 30/30 Plaza/shopping mall. On the other hand, Sammy's upbringing also influenced his decision to buy a flashy sports car with the license plate "SS 30-30," and a huge gold pendant with "30-30" engraved in it. While it took a while for Sammy to realize that he didn't need such flash to prove to the world that he had "made it," it's easy to see how someone who was raised never knowing where his next meal would come from came by such mistakes honestly.

His pendant, now safely retired to a Dominican trophy case, was certainly a source of good-natured ribbing, but it also spoke a great deal about Sammy's early experience of success. For example, Tom Verducci of *Sports Illustrated* called it a "gold millstone approximately the size of a manhole cover, hung from a chain fashioned from a suspension bridge cable." And teammate Mark Grace, when asked if Sammy wore it while playing, said, "There's no way you could run with *that* on!" Sosa's response at the time, however, was telling. "I used to watch Andujar and Fernandez," he told the *Chicago Tribune*'s Melissa Isaacson shortly after he broke into the big leagues. "They had good cars and it made me feel good thinking maybe someday I could have a car and give my mother a good house." In other words, showing off your good fortune was as important as alleviating the misfortune of others in the mind of a young man who believed in Christian salvation but was also a step away from actual starvation. Sammy had faith in God and love for his country and family—but especially with his background, he needed to be shown acceptance by management and teammates before he could completely become a team player. And when the Cubs did so, rewarding Sammy with a four-year, 42-million-dollar contract at the end of 1997, Sammy responded both on and off the field in a way that, save God Himself, no one thought possible.

Because, although Sosa's numbers had certainly improved, his critics said his stats were selfish. Sammy, writers claimed, was not a complete player and did not justify such a monster contract. Sammy seemed consistent, hitting 36 home runs and 119 runs batted in in 1995, 40 and 100 in 1996 (in only 124 games due to injury) and 36 and 119 again in 1997, but some sportswriters maintained that Sammy was actually regressing. Not only did his batting average decrease from '96 to '97 (.273 down to .251), his strikeouts increased from 134 to a whopping 174. "The worst 36 home run, 119 runs batted in season ever," Verducci deduced, while others scoffed that he merely padded his own stats at the expense of the team, and the Cubs' 68-94 record in '97 was evidence that he was not a leader. They called Sammy an overrated hot dog and nicknamed him "Sammy So-So."

But the critics—who also conveniently overlooked Sammy's growing charity work—also let the dollar signs of the new contract blind them to what this new contract *really* meant to Sosa himself. True, forty-two million dollars not only meant that Sammy and his family would never go hungry again, but also provided for all future financial needs as well. With this contract, Sammy's lot grew to ten cars, and his mom was on her third gift house—each one bigger than the last. "Last year, the pressure [from not having a new contract offer, as well as having no power hitters batting around him] made me try to hit two home runs with every at bat. But it's not easy for a Latin player to take a hundred walks," said Sosa, as Omar Minaya, the scout that discovered him, elaborated. "You have to understand something about young Latin players—or any player from a low economic background. They know the only way to make big money is by putting up big offensive numbers."

So now that he finally *had* the big money, Sammy vowed to be more patient at the plate. His '98 goals did not revolve around home runs but involved hitting .300, scoring 100 runs, and getting those 100 walks. Of course, all those hours he spent in the weight room that winter didn't figure to hurt his power numbers either.

But the real key to the long-term contract was that Sammy finally felt respected and wanted, as reflected in his comment, "If we can play like a family this year, we can win." For the first time, Sammy's extended "family" extended to the Cubbies, which that year added to their roster a potent left-handed power hitter in Henry Rodriguez, a crafty closer in Rod Beck, and a flame-throwing rookie named Kerry Wood. Feeling wanted by ownership and seeing a stronger supporting cast in place, Sammy was not only ready to roll, but grow.

Although Mark McGwire was hitting homers at an amazing pace in 1998 from the get-go, the biggest story for the Cubs during the first two months of the season was Kerry Wood's National League record twenty-strikeout performance in early May—and the fact that Chicago actually started off with a decent record. Sammy was no more than a footnote at this point, his improved team-play notwithstanding. On June 1, Sammy trailed McGwire in dingers 27-13. But that would change rapidly as the only thing Sammy did more frequently in June than homer was smile.

As many of you recent baseball historians may recall, Sammy set a major league record for homers in a month when he hit twenty in June of 1998—including eight in one week. By the end of the month, Sammy trailed the still-sluggin' McGwire by only four (37-33), and the great home run race was on.

While breaking a thirty-seven-year home run record for most round trippers in a season certainly holds interest for many baseball fans, it would not have captured the imagination of the nation without Sosa's humility and humor along the way. After his incredible June, when reporters began to ask Sosa (in addition to McGwire) if he could break Roger Maris's record of 61 HRs in a season, Sammy would say with all sincerity, "Mark is the man!" often adding, "He is my idol." As for himself, Sammy told reporters, "I just have to keep with my plan to be more patient at the plate, try to become the best player I can be, and [keep] thanking God for so much."

But if he took advantage of his chances at the plate, he really endeared himself to the fans with his "home runs" behind the mike. At one joint press conference with McGwire, Mark was on edge with the questions about pressure, when Sammy stood up and brought down the house, saying in his best Chico Esquelo accent, "I have to say, bezbol's been bery bery good to me." Still, Sammy's timely impression of the stereotyped "Saturday Night Live" Latin baseball player was nothing compared to his delivery when the 6'5", 250-pound McGwire was questioned about his use of the bodybuilding supplement Androstenedione, which was legal in baseball but banned in several other sports. When the reporters turned to Sosa and asked Sammy whether or not he used any bodybuilding supplements, a momentary hush fell over the crowd when Sammy said "yes" and went to his locker room to retrieve it. Of course, the silent anticipation was quickly replaced by howling laughter when he brought back a bottle of Flintstones Vitamins, although Sammy later added, "I don't take nothing illegal. When you got God, you don't need nothing illegal."

As the summer wore on, and both the Cubs pennant race and the home run chase got more intense, every Sosa at bat was an event. Sammy always tapped the plate three times at the beginning of a game (for the Father, Son, and Holy Spirit), but what fans really remembered was what happened after his home runs. Sammy would always hop sideways several times while watching the ball go out, then, once in the dugout, he would go right to the camera and tap his lips twice and then his heart with the index and middle fingers of his right hand. These heart-tap kisses were actually Sammy's way of sending his love back to his mom, watching in San Pedro. ("I felt like Sammy was embracing me each time he did it," she said.) Then Sammy would flash a two-fingered victory sign to Harry Caray, the beloved Cub broadcaster, also a Catholic, who died shortly before the 1998 season began, "just to let him know we're thinking about him." And with some of the Cubs' incredible comebacks that year, it was hard for Sammy—and many Chicagoans—to not believe that Harry was, indeed, up there smiling back, interceding for the team.

With a little help from his new friend, McGwire, Sammy brought baseball back from the dead. Four years earlier a strike had cancelled baseball's playoffs and World Series, and the fans had stayed away in droves. Now Sammy and "Big Mac" were playing to packed houses, and things got so crazy that opposing fans not only gave Sammy a standing ovation when he came to the plate, but booed their own pitcher when he dared to issue the Cubs' slugger a walk! In the end, both men beat Maris's record, as McGwire finished with 70 HRs to Sammy's 66, but Sosa, who finished with 158 RBIs (to lead the majors) and a .308 batting average, was named the league's most valuable player. Sammy led his team to the wild card in that wild season and, although the Cubs lost in the playoffs to the Atlanta Braves in three straight, Sammy was honored by many officials as if they had won it all.

In New York, Cardinal John O'Connor declared a special day for Sammy, first by presenting him with the Medal of John Paul II for "great sportsmanship that inspired our youth," and later by holding a parade for Sosa so his New York fans could cheer him up close. During the medal ceremony held at St. Patrick's Cathedral, Cardinal O'Connor was seen joking around with Sammy, placing a red skullcap on Sosa's head and announcing in Spanish to the large audience, "You were once a little cub, now you are a big cardinal." To the delight of the audience, Sammy laughed, too, but grew serious as he climbed the marble pulpit of the cathedral and spoke. "Through patience, hard work, and prayers, I was able to achieve something I thought I couldn't achieve," he said.

Meanwhile, back in the Dominican Republic, a national Day of Joy was declared in Sammy's honor, and the events included a thirty-mile parade from his hometown to the capital, Santo Domingo. For not only did Sammy's breaking the home run mark fill all his countrymen with great pride, it lifted their spirits during a time of great devastation. Shortly after Sammy hit home run #62, Hurricane Georges hit the Dominican Republic, causing many lost lives and millions of dollars in damage. But the amazing thing was, despite the destruction, the people did not despair, as even those left homeless continued to follow the rest of the home run race. "Sammy is giving these people something to look forward to," said Fr. Torivio Rodriguez, a priest in San Pedro de Macoris. "He's clearly a source of inspiration and hope throughout the city."

Still, although it is not something he ever seeks to publicize, Sosa was certainly honored for more than his homers, or as Dominican bishop Antonio Camilo Gonzalez put it, for "giving us [with McGwire] a great example of how competitions should take place." Sammy not only personally donated several million dollars of his own money to the hurricane relief efforts in his country, but he flew to the Dominican Republic to help distribute food and other emergency aid with his own hands. And so, no matter what you think about his politics, few could disagree with President Clinton's assessment of the Cub superstar when he singled out Sammy in his 1999 State of the Union Address, saying, "For far more than baseball, you are a hero in two countries tonight." In other words, in the minds and hearts of millions, he had gone from being "Sammy So-So" to "Sammy Claus."

○   ○   ○

Although 1999 was another banner year for Sammy, in which he nearly matched his MVP numbers of '98 (hitting .288, while smacking 63 HRs and driving in 141), the same could not be said for the Cubbies. After a fine start, the northsiders tail-spun miserably, finishing dead last with a record of 67-95. As usually happens in such situations, the Cub manager, level-headed and level-voiced Jim Riggleman (who had become one of Sammy's greatest supporters), was fired, to be replaced by brash former Colorado Rockies manager Don Baylor. And much to the surprise of the die-hard Cub fans, one of Baylor's first actions as manager was to make a public enemy out of Slammin' Sammy.

At the annual Cub Convention in January of 2000, Baylor seemingly singled out Sosa with his criticism of last year's Cub players, calling Sammy's fielding and base-stealing sub-par and, again, calling attention to the slugger's strikeouts. And indeed, at 6'0", 205 pounds, Sammy was no longer the base-stealing threat of his youth, and his fielding percentage and strikeout ratio will never be at the level of Roberto Clemente, former Hall of Fame Latin outfielder for whom Sammy picked the #21 he now wears. So, while Baylor's accusations certainly had a grain of truth in them, mentioning Sammy as a significant cause of the Cubs' collapse was like calling Mother Teresa's efforts in Calcutta a failure because thousands of Indians still died from starvation. In other words, it made little sense, especially to Sammy.

◆   ◆   ◆

If 1998 was Sosa's year to pursue McGwire, 2000 was my summer to pursue Sammy. While getting to interview a superstar of Sammy's magnitude is never easy, the groundwork for my request was laid and everything seemed to be progressing as planned, thanks to the help of Benjie de la Fuente, the Cubs' public relations guru. Still, something felt wrong. The Cubs had reverted to typical form, playing dismally right from the start—but that wasn't the problem. Sammy was having his usual good season, but his once ever-present smile seemed to be in place less and less. And then the unthinkable happened. Sammy apparently had had enough, and asked to be traded.

It was early June when Sosa spoke out, ending his silence on the Baylor situation. "From the first day he got here, he [Baylor] has been saying negative things about me for no reason . . . I don't appreciate those comments. I came here to play hard for the team and the fans who love me out there. I don't want those negative comments to get to the people who really care about me—and have them turn against me."

"It was meant as constructive criticism, not ripping him," barked Baylor in reply. Sammy's fears seemed to materialize, however, when "Trade Sosa" signs began to appear in the bleachers and Baylor continued to take his criticisms of his superstar to the media rather than to Sammy personally. But the most ironic thing about the timing of Sammy's speaking out was the fact that Cardinal

Lopez-Rodriguez of the Dominican Republic was visiting Chicago (and Sosa) that day, and Sammy brought the cardinal into the Cub dugout to meet his teammates (as well as Baylor) not long before Sammy's "talk." But in light of Lopez-Rodriguez's appearance, perhaps Sammy's response to a further question—in which a reporter asked if Sammy felt like he was being set up as a bad guy so that the Cubs' organization could justify trading him—was not unexpected.

"I cannot make everybody happy," Sammy began. "When Jesus Christ came here, He tried to make everyone happy. He's the one guy who was . . . perfect, and He couldn't do it. Everybody criticized him because he was the real Messiah. So if they criticized him, what about me? That's the way the world is."

Just when a trade appeared imminent, Sammy—whether due to the prayers of the Cub faithful, the inner workings of the Holy Spirit, or the mediocre trade bait offered by (Yankee owner) George Steinbrenner—decided he would forsake his trade request, at least for the time being, as he tried to win his dour manager over with his hard play and ready smile.

Sammy's plan worked magnificently. Not only did he manage to make Baylor a member of the Sosa fan club ("I don't put Sammy at fault at all," said Baylor after Sammy talked to his manager in private. "I wish all our players gave the effort he does every day"), but the Cubs started to win. After Sosa announced that he was going to stay on the north side, the Cubbies climbed back into the divisional race by winning 16 of 21, as Sammy was named National League Player of the Month in July for belting 11 homers and hitting nearly .400 during that span. And best of all, my interview request was back on.

Baseball, however, is a sport in which one player cannot carry a team for an entire season, so by the time my media request did come through on August 29, the Cubs had fallen off the National League Central maps, firmly back in last place. Still, with Sammy back on board, the majority of fans didn't seem to mind, and there was still joy in Cubville despite their dreadful record.

Getting off the "L" (the elevated train system in Chicago) at the Addison stop almost precisely at four o'clock, I realized that I might have to fight raindrops as well as other sportswriters for Sammy's attention. It was still nearly three hours before game time, but many of the Cubs were already on the field, stretching and taking batting practice. Several of the beat writers were already gathered around the dugout, ready to pounce on a story, any story, as I strolled onto the field, showing my press pass to a young security guard named Allison.

"Where exactly does this allow me to go?" I asked her, pointing to my pass.

"You can go anywhere in foul territory," she gestured. "Just make sure you don't go on the field."

Just being *on* the grass in Wrigley Field is certainly an experience in itself. With the possible exception of the soon-to-be-demolished Fenway Park (scheduled for the wrecking ball after the 2001 season), Wrigley is the country's most historic and revered baseball stadium and, standing on the sod, I could almost feel its sports history seeping into me. While the roof was dotted with flags commemorating former Chicago greats such as "Hack," "Tinkers," and "Ryno," I was struck by how many Cub heroes of the past were still on the grounds and walking past me, working in various capacities for the organization. For example, near the backstop was Ron Santo, former Cub third baseman-turned-radio broadcaster, scurrying around for some pre-game sound bites. And near the on-deck circle was Hall of Fame Cub outfielder Billy Williams, now a graying Cub hitting coach, dispensing grandfatherly advice about "the swing" to Gary Matthews, Jr., a second-generation Cub whose father played in a previous Cub outfield. But the Rockwell-esque mood was suddenly broken when Mr. Baylor emerged from the dugout. A nearly twenty-year player in the majors himself, Baylor was just as hard-nosed a competitor in his playing days as he is as manager. Although he won the MVP award in 1979 playing for the Angels, and amassed 338 home runs and 285 stolen bases, his intense physical style of play is best depicted by the one major league record he still holds: 267 hit-by-pitches. Moving in a little closer to the smallish circle of writers who had surrounded the manager, I could hear his replies quite distinctly. "All the guys are still playing hard . . . I haven't seen anyone cash it in . . . *yet* . . . yes, there's still a lot to play for . . . not just for next year, but, whether we're in the race or not, pride makes it important to win *now*. Winning never gets old."

○ ○ ○

"When does Sammy usually come out onto the field?" I asked my new friend Allison.

"Actually he *is* out . . . look way down in the right field corner," she pointed. "He should be by the dugout in a little while."

"So . . . is Sammy always friendly with you guys?" I wondered.

"Oh, yes. Sammy's *always* nice . . . but I can't talk about it."

"What do you mean?" I questioned.

"You see, I'm a member of security, and we're not supposed to talk to writers."

"Oh. I'm sorry."

"That's okay. You didn't know," she said reassuringly.

"Hey, what are you doing here?" asked a different but familiar voice behind me. It was Paul Meyer, the host of a local cable show (and fellow YMCA workout person), there to do a feature on the Cubs and Wrigley Field, although probably not in that order. After being there by myself for nearly an hour, it was good to be near someone I knew. Offering to give me a lift home after the game, an offer I gladly accepted, Paul then asked the inevitable question. "Did you get to talk to Sammy yet?"

"No," I replied. "He hasn't really been this way yet. Maybe I should go ask Baylor a couple of questions while I'm waiting," I decided, and walked over to my favorite security guard. "Hey, Allison . . . is it okay to go over by the backstop?" I asked, pointing to a spot behind the batting cage where the Cubs manager was standing.

"Sure. But be careful."

"I will," I smiled, not realizing that foul balls were *not* the thing she was most fearful about.

"Hello, Mr. Baylor," I started pleasantly. As he offered no reply save a stare, I decided to keep going. "My name is Tom O'Toole, and I'm writing a book for Sheed & Ward."

"Sheed & Who?" came the answer, accompanied by a glare similar to the one the Grinch gave his dog, Max, when the subject of Christmas first came up.

"Sheed & *Ward*. And I'm writing a book on Catholic athletes . . . "

"I'm *Baptist*—so I can't help you!"

"I'm actually doing a chapter on Sammy Sosa," I said, fighting to continue, "and was wondering, as you work with Sammy every day, do you ever see his faith helping him through . . . difficult situations?"

"God is a *personal* thing!" Baylor declared. "I can't say *anything* about anyone else's faith!"

"Well . . . are things going better between you and Sammy now that you two have talked things out?"

"Some *other* [reporter] started that, and I'm *not* going to say *anything* more about it!"

"Well . . . thanks for your time," I concluded, walking away a bit more briskly than when I approached. In retrospect, I can see that it must be very difficult for an extremely competitive man like Don Baylor to answer the same old questions the media puts forth every day, especially when your team is losing. On the other hand, I can also understand how a gentle soul like Sammy would have a hard time dealing with Baylor's rough exterior, at least at first—for my initial impression of Baylor was also somewhat less than charitable.

◊ ◊ ◊

"Hey, here's your chance!" said Paul as we both saw Sammy sprinting in from right field and heading for the dugout. Unfortunately, an increasing swarm of reporters descended upon the smiling superstar, and I was yet to get a word in edgewise when Sammy announced, "I gotta go back to work!" and headed toward the cage to await his turn at batting practice.

"Not quick enough," I muttered to myself as another smiling man noticed my frustrations and came up to shake my hand.

"Tom O'Toole? I'm Benjie de la Fuente."

"Benjie! It's good to finally meet you in person."

"So . . . have you got to talk to Sammy yet?"

"No," I admitted. "Maybe I can talk to him during batting practice."

"That's probably not a good idea," Benjie cautioned. "Why don't you try to catch him right after he's done?"

"Okay," I agreed, while watching Sammy laugh, talk, hit, laugh some more, hit some more. "He *always* seems to be smiling," I observed to Benjie.

"Yes, he does. He really seems to enjoy himself," he agreed, heading off to help someone else.

Well, Sammy finally finished batting, but I pretty much struck out myself. Sammy came off the field, answered a preapproved reporter's question, had his picture taken with some children, shook someone else's hand (while some preappointed person took a picture), and then sat down with yet another group of kids, smiling and signing autographs as still more cameras flashed. It was utterly amazing to watch, for I realized that all these people had prearranged appointments, the majority, like myself, waiting months for their few moments with Sammy. It was late August, the Cubs were more than twenty games out of a playoff spot, and yet Sammy's every available second when he wasn't batting or fielding was taken up with fans or media or both. When much is given, I realized, much is also expected.

It was almost six o'clock when Benjie returned to the field. Although I'm sure he could tell by my expression that I was still not successful with Sosa, he asked anyway.

"No, Benjie," was all I could say.

"Well, maybe I can help," Benjie offered. Although my press arrangement clearly stated I was only allotted "group time" with Sammy, Benjie said he would *try* to arrange a few minutes for me with him in private.

"That would be *great*!" I exclaimed.

"How many questions do you have?" Benjie inquired.

"Three, ah, how about two?"

Benjie nodded at my second number, and went to work. I, in turn, took out my Miraculous Medal and began reciting the prayer while rubbing it between my fingers.

◆   ◆   ◆

After about ten minutes, just as the sky was at its most ominous—and I was at my most nervous—Benjie reappeared from the dugout.

"He's ready, let's go," he said.

Benjie led me down the long narrow tunnel to the Cubs' locker room, but when we got to the entrance, he merely pointed at Sammy's locker and stayed behind. The room was fairly empty, and surprisingly quiet. Sammy was the only player in that quarter of the locker room. With the exception of his family and good friends, I was probably as alone with Sosa as anyone had been since early 1998.

"Hello, Sammy," I greeted, as he returned the greeting, smiling and shaking my hand. But he quickly grew serious. Benjie had informed Sammy about the nature of my inquiry, and his demeanor became very different than the joyful, exuberant one he exhibited while warming up. Sammy gave me his undivided attention as if I were the pitcher and he was up at bat.

"Sammy, is there anything about the Catholic faith— the Mass, the sacraments, devotion to saints, medals— that's especially important to you?"

Sammy thought for a second, then answered with imperfect English but perfect sincerity.

"My Catholic faith helps me to believe in God," Sammy said, looking me in the eye. "Sometimes I stop and say to myself 'I am living a dream.' I'll remember where I was; living in the Dominican Republic in a small house and working from when I am little so I have something to eat, and then I look at what I am today and say, 'Somebody up there really helped me.' Deep down I believe it was God who helped me, who gave me the strength to believe and to work hard to get this dream. So my faith helps me believe that God [not only] brought me here but [also] gave me all this, too," Sammy said, while making an expansive gesture with his hands and arms.

I looked at Sammy, then down at the sandwich by his locker, trying to decide exactly how to word the next two questions to make them sound like one.

"How has your relationship with high-profile Catholics you've met, such as Cardinal [John] O'Connor and Cardinal [Nicolas] Lopez-Rodriguez, helped you, and what advice would you give to the Catholic—and non-Catholic—kids who look up to you as a role model?"

"Cardinal O'Connor was a *great* person," Sammy started, "and I am very lucky the Lord allowed me to meet him and be around him. The greatest thing I remember about him—he just really opened his heart to me. He really went out of his way to spend time with me." Although Sammy had been with the cardinal for only a couple of days, it was as if he were recalling a lifelong friend, and the muscular outfielder's soliloquy was quite touching, especially when he began to recall the cardinal's death. "Cardinal O'Connor died a few months ago," he said looking directly at me to determine if I had heard the news, "and it's sometimes hard for me to believe he is gone." A tear was forming in Sammy's eye, but he composed himself and continued. "But I know he is in a better place, up there with God.

"Cardinal Lopez-Rodriguez?" Sammy asked himself. "He has been just unbelievable for our country. He has helped so many people in my country. A *lot* of people believe because of him. And I think it is because anybody can knock on his door." Sammy, who had again been looking down at his sandwich, looked up at me as if to emphasize his point. "You may think he talks to me just because I'm famous. But Cardinal Lopez-Rodriguez has helped lots of different people and will talk to *anyone*."

The last question (no, Sammy didn't really buy the fact that my "two-part" question was really one, but he didn't seem to mind either) took Sammy the longest to answer, for although it was certainly the most frequently asked of the three, he responded in a way that made you feel it was, to him, the most important. "First thing I say to kids is, 'Say no to drugs.' Then I tell them to honor their father and mother. And listen to your friends—your *good* friends. Not the ones who say 'yes' to everything you do, but the ones who will stand up to you and also tell you where you've done something bad. And believe in God. God is the only way you'll be safe."

For what seemed like an extremely long time, but was probably no more than six or seven seconds, there was silence. Certainly, I wanted to ask him more, to be in his presence a little longer. In my younger days, I probably would have, asking questions until someone told me to go. But being older, and having just witnessed what he had to deal with every day, I realized that would not be fair. I had gotten more time than most, and I just had to trust that my message had come across. Still, maybe there was one more thing I could leave him with.

"Thank you, Sammy, thank you so much!" I exclaimed as I got up to go. But as I extended my hand, it still held the Miraculous Medal, and I decided to give it to him to keep.

"Sammy, this is for you. It's a Miraculous Medal, the most famous of Catholic medals, for it has the most miracles associated with it. Thanks again."

As I started to walk away, Sammy took the medal and looked at it with wonder. Just before I reached the tunnel that led back out, I took one glance back to see Sammy still holding the medal, examining its inscriptions—and seemingly touched by its message. My guess from that glance was that Sammy had not seen one before, but that, from the way he looked at it, he was at least going to ask someone—perhaps Cardinal Lopez-Rodriguez—about it, if not actually wear it. And although the contrast between his unabashed joy during play and his utter seriousness while discussing his faith was probably the thing that struck me the most, his sincere gratefulness for a medal that cost around fifty cents (approximately one-millionth of what the infamous 30/30 medallion did) was certainly memorable, too. "Everyone is always *asking* him for something;

he was probably surprised to actually receive something," was my agnostic brother-in-law Gary Ohlin's completely rational explanation of the situation. But as I walked out of the tunnel, two slightly more eternal thoughts held my imagination. My first was, of course, thankfulness for the interview, but the second was whether giving Sammy the medal was the right thing to do—and whether he would actually wear it some day.

"How'd it go?" asked Paul, greeting me almost as soon as I set foot outside.

"Great, Paul. Really great," I said, as I realized one more striking fact. When I went into the clubhouse a few moments earlier, the skies were dark and cloudy—and now they were clear and sunny.

◉   ◉   ◉

"Hey, Tom! We're gonna go shoot some footage [of the ballpark] for our show. Would you like to come with us?" Paul asked.

"Sure," I said. The old ballpark looked great in the early evening, late summer sun and, with my work done, there seemed no reason not to experience it from a few different angles. Of course, any tour of Wrigley inevitably ends up in the bleachers, the destination of many a Sosa homer as well as the home of the lovable "Bleacher Bums." True, many white-collar yuppies have found it fashionable to inhabit the bleachers in the last few years, but it was early enough in the evening that only the loyal blue collar, beer-drinking, name-calling, die-hard fans (the ones who originally earned the moniker back during the Cubs' ill-fated pennant run in '69) had arrived.

The Padres were still taking batting practice and the Bums were yelling for homers, as were a number of fans outside the stadium on Waveland Avenue. While there certainly weren't as many waiting for outside homers as when Sammy was going for the record, it was still amazing that grown men, many perhaps second- or third-generation Cub fans, would stand out on the lawns of their three-flats for a few hours each night just for a chance at a major league baseball. Sure enough, one of the Padres did manage to jack one out while we were watching, and a mad scramble for the ball ensued, as these guys forsook injuries and traffic in hopes of securing the prize. Finally, a middle-aged fan with a tank top and beer belly emerged with the ball, and the small but verbal crowd cheered as he held up his souvenir.

"He's as happy as a kid!" I said to Paul's brother, Dave, who was catching the scene on film.

"Yes, I guess that's what baseball is all about—giving men a chance to be kids again," he answered.

Dave was right, at least for now, and even that had a lot to do with Sammy. For many years, sports, especially baseball, was America's way of returning to the innocence of childhood, but spiraling salaries and corrupt morals among both players and management had seriously damaged that link. But just as God always provided a saint or two to steer the Catholic Church back when it appeared to be going off course, the Lord sent Mark and Sammy to make baseball a field where boys and men can once again hope and dream.

◊   ◊   ◊

The game that night was close throughout, almost painfully so, for when the Cubs tied it to force extra innings, I knew my die-hard compatriots would not leave until the issue was resolved—and that didn't come until the thirteenth inning, when the Padre pitcher intentionally walked Sammy along with Mark Grace to get to Ricky Gutierrez, but the young Cub spoiled the ploy by singling home the winner. For the night, Sammy was 2-5 with two free passes, including a walk in which he fouled off five pitches before getting to first, something he never would have been patient enough to do three years ago.

When the clock struck midnight, we were in front of the Harry Caray statue outside the stadium as Paul was interviewing the few really, really die-hard Cub fans still milling about. Meanwhile, I was just about to fall asleep standing up. But as my eyes closed I caught a glimpse of Paul's late-night enthusiasm, and I decided Paul wouldn't still be out there working if Sammy's earlier enthusiasm for his faith had not been there to feed on.

And then I thought about my long wait to see Sammy, and the long day that had just occurred—and I knew that all my waiting would have been in vain if Sammy had not become more patient, too. For if 1998 was the year Sammy became a hero because of his triumphant Christian joy, 2000 (in which Sammy led the league with 50 HRs, drove in 138 and hit .320, his highest average ever) was the year he became a role model because of his steadfast Catholic patience. For not only is patience the first quality St. Paul writes about when describing Christian love (see 1 Corinthians 13), but the last one you are left with when tragedy strikes, and fair-weather fans abandon you for the next fad. Sammy may have been in a rush to become successful as a player, but when it comes to being baseball's ambassador of hope, the Lord seems to be in no hurry for Sammy to leave.

11. Dave Wannstedt

The Coach
Who Trusts

Trust in the Lord with all your heart,
on your own intelligence rely not.

—Proverbs 3:5

What was deemed to be a demotion for Dave Wannstedt seemed, at the same time, to be my good fortune. Reigning National Football League head coaches are among the hardest souls to pin down because even those with souls are busy trying to get an edge on their opponents. As a result, it is difficult for a writer to get a question in edgewise, let alone an interview. But I appeared to be in luck. The current season found Dave, after six years as head coach of the Chicago Bears, second banana to good friend Jimmy Johnson, serving as assistant head coach for the Miami Dolphins. Furthermore, when I called Dolphin director of media relations Harvey Greene, the current season was almost over, and he assured me that shortly after the playoffs commenced, Coach Wannstedt would love to chat with me. Instead, shortly after I talked to Mr. Greene, the bottom fell out for the entire Dolphin organization. Less than twenty-four hours after the Dolphins' disastrous 62-7 playoff loss to the Jacksonville Jaguars, Jimmy Johnson resigned, and Dave Wannstedt lost the "assistant" part of his title and was named Miami's head coach. In turn, I lost my scheduled opportunity to talk to Dave; between choosing his staff, sorting through free agents, and scouting the draft, I'm sure my interview was the least of his worries.

Dave Wannstedt grew up in Baldwin, Pennsylvania, the eldest of six children, in a strict blue-collar Catholic household. Baldwin, barely fifteen minutes from downtown Pittsburgh, is within a stone's throw of the suburbs that produced Hall of Fame quarterbacks Joe Namath, Johnny Unitas, and Joe Montana, and is also only thirty-two miles away from Aliquippa, the hometown of his Bear coaching predecessor Mike Ditka. Pittsburgh has long been known for its football fanaticism and fervent faith, and Dave was no exception, excelling first as captain of the Baldwin High Highlanders, and then for Johnny Majors' Pitt Panthers, all the while serving as an altar boy at his parish church, St. Wendelin's.

In Baldwin, faith and football are connected in another way as well: both require that you climb a hill to succeed. Baldwin High's forty-foot hill behind its east end zone had already been a source of torture and atonement for the football team, but when Dave began not only running the hill but also ascending it on all fours (carving a dusty "W" in the process), the coaches adopted the exercise for everyone, naming it the "Wannstedt Drill." Not far away, Wannstedt's church, St. Wendelin's, is on the highest hill in Pittsburgh, and Dave used to walk or jog up the hill each time he attended Mass (or the elementary school) instead of taking the easy way. Later, Dave even made his two daughters climb this hill to Mass each time he returned home for a visit—even though Custer Avenue will take your car almost the whole way there.

"I told them it was for self-improvement—but also to appreciate what I went through as a kid," Wannstedt said.

Wannstedt's playing career at Pittsburgh was stellar enough that the Green Bay Packers considered him a great candidate to plug the holes on their offensive line, drafting Dave in 1974. "Like most high draft picks, I was looking forward to playing in the NFL, and thought I would have a long pro career," Dave told me. Instead, a severe pre-season neck injury kept him out that whole year. Back in Pittsburgh the following spring to rehabilitate and re-evaluate, Dave was hoping for a callback from Green Bay or another pro team but, instead, the first inquiry of '75 came from Johnny Majors, his former coach at the University of Pittsburgh. Would Wannstedt consider becoming a graduate assistant coach on Majors' staff, while at the same time pursuing his masters? It was a tough decision for Dave, one of the first he had to pray long and hard about. "I really did want to continue playing," Dave said, "but after that neck injury, I think teams were skeptical. Green Bay and a couple of other teams did call eventually, but by then I had already made a verbal commitment to Pitt. Plus none of the pro tryouts offered guaranteed contracts, and I had just gotten married and was looking for something more stable." Thus, Wannstedt, now wed to his high school sweetheart, chose the relative comfort of furthering his education in his hometown while working for his old college coach. "I had always figured I would coach eventually," Dave explained, "and this seemed like a great way to break in."

In reality, the coaching profession offers everything but a secure position and, early on, Wannstedt wondered if he had made the right choice. After another discouraging day of teaching on the Pitt gridiron, Dave was seriously thinking of changing his career path when a fellow youthful assistant, the charismatic Panther line coach, approached Wannstedt and spoke some prophetic words.

"Don't worry about today," his coaching comrade reassured him. "You're a good teacher and you'll make a great coach. Just stick with me and you'll go places." The assistant's name was Jimmy Johnson.

As it turned out, Johnson knew what he was talking about. Not only did Jimmy convince Dave to stick with coaching, but Wannstedt stuck with Johnson for most of his career. He helped Jimmy, and Johnny Majors, coach Pitt to a national championship in 1976, then followed Jimmy to Oklahoma State, then to Miami of Florida and another number-one ranking, then to the Dallas Cowboys and two titles, and finally back again to Miami to assist Jimmy with the Dolphins. True, Wannstedt did separate himself from Jimmy on a couple of occasions: first as a non-Johnson assistant at Southern California for three seasons, and later for his head coaching job with the Chicago Bears. But they were together so often, yet outwardly so different, that they could have been called football's odd couple. Of course, if you were "Wise," you'd also know there was more to the story than that.

But more about Wise—Wannstedt's friend Tony Wise— later. The Wannstedt-Johnson relationship has been analyzed many times by the media. Wannstedt has been called the good cop to Johnson's bad cop, the calm to Jimmy's storm, the yin to his yang. In spiritual terms, though, it could be summed up like this: Johnson helped Wannstedt believe in himself as a coach, and Wannstedt helped Johnson believe in Christ as his Savior.

There can be no doubt that Johnson gave Dave confidence in his unique ability to design a defense. By the time Johnson (unlike Wannstedt, a head coach most of his career) put his Catholic friend in charge of this facet of the game at the University of Miami and later Dallas, Wannstedt's defenses almost always dominated. And when Dave's Dallas Super Bowl days came, the media deemed D. W. a defensive genius—something Johnson knew from day one.

Johnson also helped Wannstedt succeed in this stressful line of work by getting Dave to relax on occasion. For Wannstedt, who considered twelve hours of work a half-day, Johnson was the perfect tonic, with or without gin. If Dave persuaded Jimmy to make jogging sessions into coaching staff meetings, Jimmy got Dave to realize that more can sometimes be accomplished over a pitcher of beer and a plate of nachos than going over a game film for the tenth time. "If I ever wanted to cut out for a while to attend Mass, or if I had an important family function to attend, Jimmy would never hold it against me," Dave told me. "In fact, he'd encourage me to go. I'm sure that's one of the reasons our friendship is so strong."

Meanwhile, Wannstedt's influence on Johnson was never more evident than in the last couple of years. Jimmy, both loner and party goer, long admired Wannstedt's steadfast commitment to his family and, by logical extension, to his faith. If Johnson let Wannstedt escape from work on the rare occasion Dave would allow himself to be excused, it was because Jimmy knew that not only was Dave always up to something good, he always returned recharged and even more ready to go. But before the 1999 season began, not only did Johnson again desire the defensive skills of his ex-soulmate (exiled for six years in Chicago), he demanded it, telling Dolphin owner Wayne Huizenga that he would resign unless Wannstedt was at his side. And the playing field was perhaps the least of Jimmy's reasons for wanting Dave near.

"Dave can look across the room, read Jimmy's face, and know exactly what he's thinking," said Wannstedt's wife, Jan, in an earlier interview, explaining the reason Johnson has long liked her husband as his number-one coaching assistant. "The best thing we have going is that when we're together, we *enjoy* being together," Dave added. But Wannstedt was much closer to the truth for their recent reunion when he stated, "Jimmy knows I have no ulterior motive in coming here [as his assistant]. He knows he can trust me."

Since Wannstedt left for Chicago, trust was the one thing that Johnson was missing. Jimmy had won without Wannstedt, winning a third Super Bowl title with the

Cowboys in 1995—but Johnson was subsequently dismissed by Dallas owner Jerry Jones over a clash of egos. True, Johnson landed on his feet by grabbing the head coaching job at Miami but, by the end of 1998, his world would begin to crumble. On December 20, Johnson's mother died and, because the Dolphins had a critical game that week which would determined whether or not they made the playoffs, Jimmy did not attend her wake. During that same period, Johnson's father underwent chemotherapy (and his two kids wondered why he hadn't seen his father in months), while his girlfriend of nearly ten years, Rhonda Rookmaker, questioned his lack of commitment to her. By the time January rolled around, with all these relationships needing attention, Johnson was ready to walk away from the game forever.

But then, almost miraculously, Wannstedt became available to work, and things began to turn around. After his mother passed away, Johnson realized that life was about "being with people you care about, and not short-changing them." With Wannstedt again on board, Jimmy was able to spend more time away from the job, to be with his dad and his children, because he now had someone who cared about *him* on the job, someone he could trust. And not just on the job, for on July 17, 1992, he was finally able to tie the knot with longtime fiancée, Rookmaker, with Wannstedt, of course, by his side as best man.

But if Johnson was a fiery general in search of a trusty lieutenant, Tony Wise was a wisecracking uncle in search of a caring family. "I guess it is kind of odd in a way that, as a committed Catholic family man, my two best friends [until Johnson's recent marriage] are single Protestant guys," Dave explained. "Jimmy would let me break away to attend Mass or a family function, but Tony would often attend these things with me." Wannstedt stopped to ponder, then continued. "Tony and I would talk about faith once in a while . . . and though he never expressed a desire to become Catholic, he attended both of my daughter's first Communion Masses, and he usually goes to Christmas Mass with us. And Tony hasn't missed a Thanksgiving dinner in eighteen years."

Wise could be called the last of the three musketeers, and in his mind the least talented. (On the other hand, he considered himself the most humorous.) "I was a second-team guard from Ithaca [College] who couldn't get a high school job. Dave was a major college player and a high pro draft pick," Wise said in summarizing his expertise when he joined Johnson and Wannstedt on the University of Pittsburgh staff in 1977. "I think Jackie Sherrill [Pitt's head coach at the time] hired me because he thought I was pretty funny . . . a bit of a court jester," Tony added.

Jimmy and Dave must have thought so, too, because the quick-witted Wise followed them to Oklahoma State, the University of Miami, and Dallas, and when Wannstedt accepted the head coaching job in Chicago, Tony became Dave's assistant head coach—but not without a hilarious struggle.

As soon as Wannstedt accepted the Chicago job, Dave asked Wise's advise about every assistant coaching position except offensive line—which happened to be Tony's specialty.

"I think it was denial," said Jan Wannstedt. "I don't know if Dave was waiting for Tony to ask, or if Tony was waiting for Dave, but neither of them brought it up." Finally, after cracking open a couple of beers at the Wannstedt home, Wise "volunteered" in his usual wise-cracking way.

"Well, I guess I've *got* to come to Chicago now," Wise sighed.

"Why is that?" asked Wannstedt.

"Because I can't let you go up there without me and screw things up!" Wise replied.

"Oh yeah? Well if *that's* how you feel, *forget* about coming! There *is* no job for you in Chicago!" Dave yelled, mad as . . . heck.

"Fine!" said Tony. "I don't want one anyway!" he added, storming out.

Tony went home, and Dave went to bed. But that was not the end of the story. "I couldn't sleep, so finally I got up and drove over to Tony's house in my shorts and T-shirt," Dave recalls. "When I knocked, Tony was practically at the door already. He had been waiting for me in his living room. So we talked."

"Was it a . . . heated discussion?" I wondered.

"Yeah, a little bit. But in the end, we settled things, and Tony was my new offensive line coach."

Of course, once Wannstedt actually became the head coach of the Bears, Wise was quickly promoted to his top assistant. Because, if the positive Wannstedt was good for the admittedly cynical Wise's soul, Tony was to become the memory function in Dave's mind—whenever Dave needed to remember anything with the exception of football.

"Once when we were in the car together," Tony related, "Dave blurted out 'I never pay attention when I'm driving.' I thought I was hearing things, but Jan later told me, 'That sounds pretty accurate. He once called me on the car phone driving home from Lake Forest [the Bears practice facility] and asked 'Where am I? I took a wrong turn.'" But if that wasn't bad enough, Dave once turned to Tony while the two were jogging and asked, "Hey, Tony, how old am I?"

So if Wise needed the stability of being part of Wannstedt's family, Dave needed Tony to keep tabs on the other things in life besides football. "I have no idea why

Tony still does things like invite me out to dinner," Dave said, noting that he'll order a drink, an appetizer, and then want to leave, whereas Tony will ask for a seven-course meal followed by a cigar. "But I can sum up our relationship in three words: I trust him."

Thus, when Wannstedt became an NFL head coach at the tender age of forty, trust was the one thing he hoped to build his team upon. "My father always told me to work as if everything depended upon you, then to pray as if everything depended upon God," Dave confided.

"Ah . . . the famous St. Ignatius of Loyola quote," I said.

"Is that who said it?" Dave asked me. "Well that has also always been one of my mottos, and I think it applies even more when you become the head coach, and the final decision does depend upon you." You could almost say that Wannstedt put his philosophy into overdrive; not only did his legendary work habits increase, but his desire to seek Christ did also.

"I've read in several publications that you attend Mass every day, Dave. Is that true?" I wondered.

"Yes," Dave confided.

"Have you been going to daily Mass throughout your coaching career or did it happen gradually?"

"To be honest, Tom, I really didn't start going regularly until I came to Chicago. I was passing St. Mary's every day on the way to work, and when I realized their 6:30 a.m. Mass was right before I was arriving at Lake Forest and fit in perfectly with my work schedule, I started to go."

"The *Catechism of the Catholic Church* calls the Mass 'the source and summit of the Christian life,' 'the sum and summary of our faith,' while St. Augustine called it 'the daily bread' Christ talked about in the Our Father. Why is this experience so important for you?"

"For me, it's thirty minutes of peace, the best way to spend quiet time with Christ before the hectic day. At Mass, I give thanks to God, and it helps me see the day's problems from a spiritual standpoint. I come out of there with confidence that with His help and the help of my staff, I can accomplish what needs to be accomplished."

And in his beginning with the Bears, Wannstedt did just that. Not only was Dave attending daily Mass before his marathon work days, but Bear assistant coaches Danny Abramowicz, Mike Shula and Dave McGinnis also went to the 6:30 a.m. liturgy, a practice unparalleled in the annals of NFL coaching. Meanwhile, Dave's team began to play inspired ball as well. After finishing 5-11 (Ditka's last year) in '92, Wannstedt's Bears improved to 7-9 in '93 and 9-7 in '94, then defeated the highly favored Minnesota Vikings in their wild card playoff game before losing to the eventual Super Bowl champions, the 49ers. The Bears were back! The league voted Wannstedt the NFL Central Division Coach of the Year, and nearly everyone, from players to coaches to media types, were raving about Dave. But just as was the case with Christ, Wannstedt's public acclaim did not last.

After flying out of the blocks in '95 with a 6-2 start, a couple of key injuries hit the Bears and they leveled off to finish 9-7 again, especially disappointing in that this time that record was not good enough to make the playoffs. Then in 1996, Chicago slipped back to 7-9. After four years, Wannstedt's record was now 32-32, and Dave was called just another .500 coach. But the worst was yet to come.

Actually, 1996 started out bright. The Bears opened the season by beating the Super Bowl champion Dallas Cowboys 35-18 before a national Monday Night Football audience, and Wannstedt felt "we were finally ready to make a run at the Super Bowl. And then Eric Kramer goes and breaks his neck."

But if '96 was a disappointment, 1997 was a disaster. Bear trainer Fred Caito called it the worst in his thirty years as far as injuries go. At one time, there were eighteen Bear starters on injured reserve. And, of course, a rash of injuries often leads to seemingly rash personnel decisions, especially in the case of the Bears' move to bring in a mobile Rick Mirer to replace the fragile Kramer at quarterback. Unfortunately while Rick retained his ability to scramble that once made him a hero under the Golden Dome, Mirer lost all ability to throw the medium-length pass with touch, and the season was pretty much lost. Going with patchwork lineups almost every week, Wannstedt's Bears went 4-12 in 1997 and, when Chicago duplicated that feat in 1998, Dave's days in the Windy City were numbered.

While there are several main reasons Wannstedt's teams did *not* continue to win, it was certainly not due to a lack of effort or preparation on the part of Dave or his coaches. "Nobody is better at preparing his team every week than Dave Wannstedt," said former Bear assistant coach Joe Brodsky. "He has an outstanding work ethic, and the way he kept his kids fighting at such a high level [with a losing record] is amazing. With other teams I've coached in those situations, we just packed it in."

In the end analysis, excessive injuries and unfortunate personnel decisions—both through free-agency and the draft—contributed equally to the Bears' downfall. Certainly, any football coach would be challenged with eighteen starters strolling the sidelines on injured reserve, but the lack of impact players brought in by the Bears during the Wannstedt era is nothing less than a glaring failure for the once glorious franchise. Dave must "bear" some responsibility for the futility of such high profile free agent picks as Rick Mirer, Brian Cox, and Carlos Huerta, but as Wannstedt was neither the first nor the last man in the personnel decision chain of command, his impact on deciding which players he went to war with was minimal. So while many agreed with former all-pro linebacker and current NFL commentator Matt Millen when he said, "I watch an awful lot of games, and the Bears are as fundamentally sound as any team in the league," Millen went on to conclude, " . . . the reason they don't win more is simply because Dave doesn't have enough [talent]." The fact that the Bears did not have even one Pro-Bowl player during Wannstedt's tenure bears this out.

The other thing Wannstedt was unfairly criticized about in Chicago was that he wasn't "mean," that he didn't rant and rave and, therefore, wasn't tough enough on his players. While it is true Wannstedt never visibly disciplined his players on the sidelines a la Mike Ditka or Jimmy Johnson, Jim Flanagan, star lineman for the Bears, rightly summed up Wannstedt's way: "Dave doesn't spout off when the cameras are rolling, but he doesn't hesitate to let his players know when they are not performing either."

In asking Dave about his motivational tactics, he was quite clear about his coaching approach.

"I tried hard to never berate players in public, because I truly believe to do so is counterproductive to the player and an ego trip for the coach," Dave delineated. "You have kids, don't you, Tom?"

"Yes I do, Coach."

"I'm sure you try not to yell at them in public, but say what needs to be said when you get home."

"That's right," I agreed.

"Well, I believe that rule should also apply to men. Believe me, stuff has happened behind closed doors in the locker room [Wannstedt once winged a chair and smashed his $3,000 Rolex after an eight-turnover loss to Arizona], but by not criticizing my players in front of sixty thousand fans, I was showing my respect for them as men, and treating them as I would have wanted to be treated. And the press *really* criticized me for that."

"Yes, they did," I recalled sadly. For as it turned out, Wannstedt's demise coincided with the rise of sports talk radio in Chicago. So not only did Dave have to endure the daily second guessing of the print media like his predecessors, he was subjected to the almost hourly "Wanny" watches by the radio shock jocks. But to the bitter end, Wannstedt, who proclaimed "my unwavering faith in God is bigger than all this stuff," kept his cool. He continued to treat the press with the dignity that they rarely deserved. "No matter how much I demeaned his coaching he remained unfailingly civil to me," admitted WSCR radio host Dan Bernstein, one of his harshest critics. As a result, Dave not only remained above reproach but put himself in line to become head coach again two years later despite his six-year 41-57 record.

"I'm thankful for my years in Chicago and all the positive things that happened to my family there," Dave explained. "My wife taught religion class in Chicago and I was involved in a lot of community things, both Christian and non-Christian, that gave us a lot of joy. And as far as the losing goes . . . that's where faith comes in. You put in hours and hours of time with the team and the coaches, and yet in the end you wonder how much you, as a head coach, really have control over, and the answer is, not much. You can't control the injuries, the bad breaks, or the field goals that a few feet the other way would have won the game."

"So looking back, even losing was a positive," I said.

"It is in handling losing that you show your true character," Dave explained. "You see those who are truly loyal to the team, and those who aren't."

"I'm sure you prayed before each game, but did you ever say a quick prayer when your team was in a tight spot, for success on a certain play . . . and it worked?"

"Sure I did," laughed Wannstedt, "but it seemed like especially the last two years [in Chicago] the results were even worse when I did."

"Besides daily Mass, was there anything else you did spiritually to help get you through those seasons?"

"I also attended a weekly Bible study," Dave said. "Reading Scripture helped me keep my job in perspective, to remember Christ's view of things versus the worldly way of looking at them."

"As a coach, were there Bible verses that stuck out, that you really felt applied to you?"

Wannstedt thought for a second. "Proverbs 3:2-5— 'Trust in the Lord with all your heart . . .'"

Someone else quoted that same verse when I asked them that question, I thought to myself. Now who was it? Of course! It was Lou Holtz. "That's wild, Dave," I said. "I mean, I asked that question to Lou Holtz a few years ago, and he gave me that exact verse!"

"Is that right?" Wannstedt inquired with interest.

"Yes, well . . . you've coached *against* Notre Dame, both at Southern California and at Miami, including that 31-30 last-second Irish victory in South Bend which helped propel them over the Hurricanes for the national championship that year. Did you ever think about what it would be like to coach at Notre Dame, where Catholicism can actually be an implicit part of coaching football?"

"Yes, I have," Dave admitted. "I know several people at Notre Dame, and was up there just last summer. I went to Mass and visited the Grotto that day, and it did occur to me that it would be a special place for a Catholic to play— or coach."

When Holtz left Notre Dame, Wannstedt was actually mentioned as a possible replacement, but fate has kept Dave in the pros, albeit coaching a Dolphin team with a little Catholic tradition of its own.

"One of your predecessors in Florida, Hall of Fame coach Don Schula, was a daily Masser during his twenty-five-year Dolphin tenure. Have you reflected on the fact that Miami may have the longest running Catholic coaching tradition of any NFL team?"

"I knew Shula was a strong Catholic . . . but I haven't really thought about that part of being here."

"But you're happy about the way things turned out?"

"Yes. I mean, sure, like anyone, I would have liked to have won more with the Bears, but I have no regrets about anything I did in Chicago."

"Almost everyone I talk to for this book says how hard it is to coach and be a family man, and yet almost everyone I talked to about you says what a wonderful husband and father you are. Was it ever difficult for you to balance those two full-time jobs, especially when you were head coach?"

Suddenly, Dave's demeanor seemed to change. "Yes, Tom, it was very hard . . . in fact, to be perfectly honest with you, I *do* have one regret about my stay in Chicago, and that was that I didn't spend enough time with my family. I guess you could say I'm pretty compulsive when it comes to football, and sometimes I would get so consumed with work that I wouldn't spend the right amount of time with my girls and my wife." Dave paused. "Sometimes I'd spend hours and hours in the office or the film room looking for that one thing about your opponent that would give you the edge that week, and sometimes you wonder if it was worth it, if sometimes you're not better off knocking off and heading home."

With his last words, something instantly clicked into my own head. I thought about the night before, how I stayed late at the library, searching the web for that one fact that would give me that one great question that would make my interview with Wannstedt better than everyone else's. Later, on the way home, I found my wife and daughter walking home, in heavy rain, from an extracurricular activity. Jeanette had told me earlier that day that the second car wouldn't start, to pick them up in case of inclement weather—but in the midst of my search for perfection, I had completely forgotten.

"Maybe, Dave, sometimes you do find that extra edge, but you end up finding it at home with them."

"I think you're right, Tom. Hey, thanks for the interview. I gotta get back to my staff now . . . "

"Thank you, Coach," I ended. Sure I would have liked for the interview with Dave to be longer, but sometimes length of conversation is not as important as what's said. For in the short time that we had talked, he had given me that one answer I had been searching for—that while working late can lead to greatness, going home is "the greatest" (see I Corinthians 13:13) thing of all.

12. Thérèse of Lisieux and Tara Lipinski

The Little Flower and Her Little Friend

One day, (my sister) Leonie . . . came to us with a basket filled with (dolls, saying), "Here, my little sisters choose" . . . and after a moment's reflection, I said "I choose all!" and I took the whole basket . . .

This little childhood incident sums up my whole life . . . Later, I understood that to become a saint, one has to suffer much . . . so when Our Lord asked me to choose among all the sacrifices . . . I cried out "My God I choose all!"

—St. Thérèse of Lisieux from *Story of a Soul*

"Hello?"

"Hello . . . Tara Lipinski?" I asked. After months of hard work securing this phone interview, I could hardly believe that the operator's claim—that I was connected with the young champion—was correct.

"Yes, this is Tara."

"Tara, this is Tom O'Toole, the writer scheduled to interview you about your Catholic faith and friendship with St. Thérèse. Tara, before we get started, I wanted to tell you how much I, too, am devoted to St. Thérèse. We named our daughter Therese in answer to a prayer to her when my wife thought she couldn't conceive. In fact, this interview request was initially turned down. Then I said a five-day novena to her and, on the last day, I got a call saying the request was approved."

"That's really cool," Tara responded. "I say five-day novenas to St. Thérèse all the time. Now . . . who did you say you were again?"

Indeed, with her schedule (and my excitement), Tara Lipinski can be forgiven in forgetting the reason for my call. As the youngest figure skater ever to win the Olympic Gold Medal, Tara is, as they say in the business, "hot property," and for every interview granted, scores more are refused. But as mine was arranged with the heavenly help of a "mutual friend," it seemed only fitting that my article should focus on the relationship of Tara and Thérèse.

Tara, who was named after the plantation in *Gone with the Wind*, was a very happy and very *active* girl right from the start. At age two, Tara's Olympic dream began in two ways. She watched her first Olympic games on TV—and promptly gathered up flowers and ribbon and stood on a Tupperware container to imitate the winner. Then, later that same year, she went skating—roller-skating—for the first time.

Lipinski would go on to claim over fifty trophies and plaques for her roller-skating skills, and was one of the leading scorers in a roller-hockey league for *boys* before a hand injury brought that activity to an end. But a friend of Tara's mom, perhaps realizing that tiny Tara didn't have the size or the temperament to be a roller-derby queen, kept urging her to try ice-skating. Initially, Tara's mother, Patricia, rejected this suggestion, the nearest ice rink being over an hour away. But when Patricia finally relented, she was actually relieved to see Tara falling all over the place, figuring that her daughter would give up the new game.

But in the time it took Patricia and her husband, Jack, to go to the snack bar and drink a cup of hot chocolate, Tara had mastered the blades and was doing jumps and spins to the amazement of the cheering crowd. Well, Tara's parents *did* sign her up for ice-skating lessons, and the rest, as they say, is history.

When Tara was nine years old, her father got a job promotion that moved the Lipinskis to Houston. Then, after attending Mass at a new church one Sunday, Tara came face to face with a statue of the Little Flower. "I was first attracted to her because of her smile, and she seemed closer to my age," Tara recalled.

"Plus . . . she was on a platform and holding flowers," I interjected.

Tara laughed. "Well, she did have roses."

Despite the Little Flower's slight physical stature, Tara—herself only around five feet tall—certainly picked a giant among saints to emulate. Noting that many of the trials and triumphs in Thérèse's life mirror her own, Tara is especially quick to point out that they both dramatically defied the odds by reaching their goals at the tender age of fifteen: Tara by winning the Olympic Gold, and Therese by becoming a Carmelite nun. In fact, Tara talks so much about the help of the saint who promised us "she would spend her time in heaven doing good upon earth," that some have wondered if Tara Lipinski is giving Thérèse of Lisieux the honor due to God alone. "I try to follow God in everything I do," Tara says humbly, "but Jesus was perfect. It's nice to know someone who was like you, who experienced some of the same things and made some of the same mistakes, but then became a saint, to help you along the way. I'm not saying St. Thérèse is the right saint for everyone, but there is a saint out there whose life was similar to yours, who is there waiting to help you."

"You seem to know a fair amount about Thérèse," I told Tara.

"Well, I've been trying to read more about her . . . now that the Olympics are over, I have a little more time . . . "

"Actually, I just read something about St. Thérèse in the regular newspaper," I mentioned to Tara to see if she'd pick up on the topic.

"Yes!" Tara exclaimed, perking up even more than usual. "Pope John Paul named her a Doctor of the Church! Wasn't that cool?"

"Yes, it was," I agreed. "And I guess that would make her the youngest Doctor of the Church, too . . . if not the smallest . . . "

"How tall was St. Thérèse?" Tara suddenly asked. Having so many things in common with her friend/saint, she no doubt wanted to see how she measured up in this respect as well but, unfortunately, this question caught me by surprise.

"You know, I'm not sure, Tara. I've read several books about her . . . and they all mention that she was 'slight'— but I've never come across her actual height. I'll have to check on that one for you."

"I'd like that," she said.

"Okay. So in your St. Thérèse reading . . . did you happen to read her autobiography *Story of a Soul*?"

"I'm reading that right now!" Tara said, quite enthusiastically. "I'm almost finished with it."

"Is there any passage that really sticks out in your mind—perhaps a favorite of yours?"

"I'm not sure," said Tara, thinking. "I like it all so far . . . I know! Remember when Thérèse was little and her sister brought in a basket and told her to choose one toy—and Thérèse said 'I choose all!' and took the whole basket."

"Yes," I said with a smile, recalling that same account.

"That's me exactly!" said Tara. "When I go to the store, I never want to buy just one stuffed animal or dress or whatever; I want to buy them all. Or when I have a night off and people suggest several things to do, I always want to do all of them."

"As I recall, St. Thérèse also applied that incident to her adult life, something to the effect that when God asked her about which way she wanted to become a saint, she chose all the ways to become holy, too."

"There are a lot of things I want to do with my life in the future, too!" said Tara. "But right now I still have a lot of skating to do. I have quite a bit to learn still for my next show . . . "

And so, while Tara's instructors were the ones who taught (and are still teaching) her to skate correctly, it was St. Thérèse who inspired her to skate joyfully. "Thérèse called prayer 'an upward leap of the heart . . . a cry of gratitude and love which I utter from the depths of sorrow as well as the height of joy!'" I stated. "Unlike some skaters who give sensual or athletic performances, your skating, like Thérèse's 'leaps of the heart,' seem to exude joy. Is that because you make skating a prayer?"

"Well, I do pray before a performance that people who watch will come to believe and have faith in God. And I *do* skate from the heart. But I don't think about [being joyful] when I'm skating . . . I guess I'm just aware of all the hard work that went into my routines, so when it goes well, it just shows," Tara paused reflectively, then began again. "You know, no one, except my family and coaches, believed in my chances for gold at the Olympics. And then on the morning of my final program, a dozen roses arrived at my door."

"Roses are a sign of St. Thérèse answering prayers."

"Yes. I have gotten roses before, but this time they weren't signed. But I *knew* who they were from, and that *she* believed in me, and it helped me to skate with confidence . . . and win the gold medal."

Besides her skating, going to Mass and making hospital visits are two things that make Tara a true champion of the faith. "I love the warm welcoming feeling I get when attending Mass," said Tara, noting that not only does she go every Sunday, but tries to refrain from training that day as well. "Church helps me to feel grounded—even when I'm constantly jetting off to competitions and appearances."

"What do you think makes the Mass so special—as opposed to going to ecumenical services or just praying?"

"I think it is holy Communion," Tara answered astutely. "I like the whole liturgy, but holy Communion is my favorite part."

"Mine too," I said. But suddenly feeling that answer wasn't enough, I launched into a bit of history to make my point to Lipinski. "You mentioned holy Communion being important—did you ever hear the story of the eucharistic miracle at Lanciano?"

"No," said Tara, sounding intrigued.

"Well, around the year 700, there was this priest who kept doubting that when he consecrated the bread and wine at Mass, that they really were transformed into Christ's body and blood. But he wanted to believe, so he prayed, and one day, when he lifted up the host, it turned into a real piece of flesh, and the wine became real human blood."

"Really?" Tara asked with interest.

"And that flesh and blood has been preserved until this very day," I told her. "Not long ago, scientists tested the flesh to see if it was really human—and it was—but guess which part of the body it was from?"

"I don't know . . . the hand?" guessed Lipinski.

"No, the heart!"

"I was going to say that," said Lipinski, always the competitor.

"I guess I thought you'd like that story, Tara, because people say you skate from the heart, and you also like receiving holy Communion—for if skating is your way of giving your heart to others, perhaps the Eucharist is Jesus' way of giving his heart to you."

"That's a great way to think about Communion," Tara agreed. "Thank you for telling me about it."

As for her hospital visits, Tara calls them a "reality check."

"I realize when I'm there not only how lucky I've been, but that missing a jump is not the end of the world," Tara confided. "So many people cheer me on the ice, I look at it as my time to do some cheering."

"Cheering?" I wondered.

"Yes . . . cheering up! I used to be nervous when I went to visit kids there, but then I realized my size was an advantage. The kids would look at me, and it was like I was one of them! In fact, I'm so small, a lot of them don't even believe me at first when I say that I'm an Olympic athlete! But even after they see my picture and know I'm not kidding, they still feel comfortable talking with me, which is cool."

The "little way" strikes again, I thought.

And yet, among fellow writers, Tara's faith has many critics who say her talk of roses and religion is mere superstition, and that her life is too sheltered by wealth to have true impact on the underprivileged. In response, one has to answer that Tara is, at sixteen, still growing (and growing eagerly, I might add) in her knowledge of the faith; but that is exactly how it should be. In fact, when Tara said, "I go to Mass and tell myself that I'm going to remember every word of the readings and homily . . . but then my mind drifts so I just say a short prayer to St. Thérèse to help me remember what's important," she echoes the words of St. Thérèse herself, who said, "There are so many beautiful prayers that I get a headache reading them all, so I tell God very simply what I want and He always understands."

As for those who write that Tara's "carefree" life has made her unable to sympathize with those who suffer, I can tell you that any athlete who has worked through the physical and mental pain of training eight hours a day knows that such claims are ludicrous. Just as St. Thérèse was a "prisoner of Carmel," Tara has her own "cloisters," not only a prisoner of the ice, but often shut up in hotel rooms, awaiting the endless competitions, separated from her family and friends. I recalled to Tara the gospel passage where Christ told Peter, "When you were young, you fastened your belt and went where you pleased, but when you are old, a stranger will bind you and carry you off where you do not want to go" (John 21:18–19), and then asked her if, in her following of Christ, she now felt "old, carried off against her will."

"Well, dealing with all the training, tutoring, and media is hard sometimes," she admitted. "But it's not more than I can handle. I need all these people, not only my coaches and tutors, but my fans to cheer me and the writers to write about me. And I need you to write about and spread my devotion to St. Thérèse."

"Why, thank you Tara," I said, quite touched.

"Thank *you*."

So, while my mission to spread Tara's devotion to Thérèse is nearly finished, one last task regarding Ms. Lipinski remains. And that is to remind you that, as Tara's Catholic fans, it is essential that you now not only root for her continued success on skates, but also pray for her continuous growth in Christ. Figure skating may appear glamorous, but with skaters sending hit men to take out rivals, and medal winners abdicating their position as role models by posing between the pages of *Playboy*, it's a tough world as well and, despite all of her accomplishments, Tara is still a teen. Still, with your prayers, Tara's joyful determination, and a few more of Thérèse's roses, there's little doubt that some day Tara will follow the Little Flower in the most important way: that of becoming a saint. At least, judging by her favors to her favorite skater, "Coach" Thérèse sure thinks so.

○   ○   ○

This ended my first article written on Tara Lipinski (and Thérèse of Lisieux). It was done for another publisher, and was conducted some two years ago. Granted, when the great body of an athlete's career is behind them, two years becomes insignificant, a mere "watch in the night." But when your subject goes from sixteen to eighteen during those years, a follow-up is essential. Yet, in Tara's case, it was not to be.

Several things disturbed me in my next attempt to talk with Tara. First, a Catholic magazine that originally agreed to run my piece on Lipinski changed its mind. Second, my actual tracking of Tara became a year-long coast-to-coast misadventure, with Lipinski initially being represented by Jennifer Glasik's Agency in New York City, then by Robert Thorne in Los Angeles, and finally by Michael Pagnotta, also on the West Coast. Although striking out on an interview attempt with an athlete, especially when requesting a glimpse of their spiritual side, is nothing new or unusual, this time I got the impression that my request never actually reached Tara's hands. If it had, it seems she would have granted me a few minutes to give an update on her dealings with Thérèse ("and I need *you* to write about my devotion . . . ")—unless the critics were right . . .

"We never run a feature on a Catholic actor or actress's faith life until they're dead," said a Catholic editor, offering a possibility for why my original piece on Tara and Thérèse was not published. "With what goes on in Hollywood," he went on to note, "we have found it's just not a safe bet until they are buried."

While that certainly sounded a bit too cynical to suit my taste, I also noticed that he said "actress" not "athlete." In the subsequent two years, Tara had supplemented her skating accomplishments with some acting roles . . . but could that have really been the reason?

I looked at Tara's made-for-television resumé to see what showed up. Certainly her appearances in *Ice Angel* (Fox Family Channel movie) or guest spot on *Touched by an Angel* were harmless, and her appearance with Mike Ditka and others on the hilarious Charles Schwab commercial was unobjectionable . . . but what about her role as "Marnie, the feisty intern" on the soap opera, "The Young and the Restless"? Soap operas are not traditionally paragons of Christian virtue, and rarely espouse moral views anything close to Catholic doctrine—but I must confess I never saw Tara's soap role personally (failing in several attempts to sit through the hour-long immorality play to catch a glimpse of Lipinski's character). So I went to the expert to see if her role on "Restless" actually compromised Lipinski's role model status.

"Hello . . . Guy?"

"Yeah, this is Guy. Who the— "

"This is Tom O'Toole. How ya' doin'?"

"O'Toole, how's your book going?" Guy Lazzaro was the area's leading critic of daytime drama, having watched four or five soaps a day for decades. If anyone could give me the lowdown on Lipinski's performance, it was Guy.

"Not bad, Guy—in fact, that's why I called you. You still watching 'The Young and the Restless'?"

"Are you kidding? That's one of my favorites. I've only missed about forty episodes in twenty-seven years—most of those during my triple bypass."

"Good. I need to know about Tara Lipinski's character on that show . . . "

"She played Marnie . . . she was an intern . . . " said Guy, jogging his memory.

"But what kind of a character was she?"

"She had a pretty minor role. Tara was only on a handful of shows."

"Yes, but was she . . . you know?"

"Was she sleeping with anyone? Naw . . . Marnie mostly hung out at the coffee shop and talked to her friends, that kind of stuff."

"But she wasn't out praying or volunteering at soup kitchens either."

"No . . . It was like an extended cameo. They have a lot of those on 'The Young and the Restless' . . . I remember Wayne Gretzky had a role years ago."

"So nothing really immoral about her character?" I asked, double-checking.

"No, no whoring around or nothin'. Don't worry! She was nice. Say, when are you gonna take me out to dinner?"

"As soon as I get this book done. Thanks, Guy."

Getting the decisive word from Mr. Lazzaro made me feel confident that even in the often compromising world of daytime drama, Tara had kept her promise to her mom "to be a good girl and make sure you're a good role model for all those kids." Indeed, you had to admit that Tara at least tried her best on this front, for in addition to her frequent hospital visits, she had become a regular volunteer for the Boys and Girls Clubs of America, calling them a "great place for kids to get a chance to try everything and see what they are good at"—the highlight being when Tara helped teach a blind girl to skate.

It is one thing to fly joyfully around the ice as a fourteen- and fifteen-year-old pixie, but quite another story after you've become a beautiful young lady. At eighteen, Lipinski was not only a woman, but a professional, having forsaken her "amateur" status to become the main draw in the touring troupe Target Stars on Ice. Thanks to her presence, the Target Stars inked a multi-million dollar, thirty-year deal with International Management Group. Barring serious injury, this guaranteed that Lipinski, who was the youngest ever to win the World Championship (at fourteen) and the Olympic Gold Medal (at fifteen), would be skating until she was fifty. While becoming a perpetual professional certainly put future Olympic competitions in legal doubt, there were still the professional championship competitions.

⊙   ⊙   ⊙

The world professional championships were about to be aired and I noticed from *TV Guide* that most of the big names in women's skating were scheduled to compete. Denise Bielmann, Surya Bonaly, and Oksana Baiul were all talked about as favorites, with Tara still a possibility— although as the announcer noted, "she was still recovering from a hip injury. After all," the commentator continued, "she has grown three or four inches since the Olympics."

"Three or four inches?" I thought to myself. I remembered how I had taken Tara's question about St. Thérèse's height to the Carmelite Retreat Center in Darien, Illinois, and was told by their research staff that the Little Flower was 5'3¼". Could it be that, along with the countless youthful experiences Tara had talked about, she now shared Therese's adult height, too?

Having not seen her once-famous relationship with Thérèse written about in the previous two years, the thought still crept into my mind that perhaps Tara *had* lost the habit of talking to her Carmelite friend. "A dragon lives forever, but not so little girls," my editor acquaintance had warned me, paraphrasing a popular folk song. Could it be that in growing up, Tara had lost the "little" way, too?

Tara skated, and skated with as much grace and joy as ever, although she seemed even more "filled with grace" in comparison to the competition. "It's so refreshing to see a routine without all that bumping and grinding," the commentator declared, and the judges agreed, awarding Lipinski first place. But it was not a medal or trophy or even the flowers she picked up that I noticed most. It was a little statue of a woman that she had next to her blade protectors on rink's edge that Tara kissed right before she went on to perform, and now held in her hand. The camera provided no close-up, but I could see the figure just long enough and clearly enough to discern a little band of white by the head and a little circle of red roses by the figure's hand. Tara smiled, and I smiled back at the set, for I once again knew that in Lipinski's case, the prayers of the Little Flower and the Catholic faithful had prevailed.

But Tara is still young, so I will keep praying—praying and rooting for her continued success on the ice and her vocational choices away from it—although there is one little thing I ask in return. If, Tara, on one of your breaks from skating, someone approaches you to play the lead in a film about the life of St. Thérèse of Lisieux, please take it. Because, from all my research on the subject, I know you would be perfect for the role.

Alberto Salazar

The Marathon Man and His Inspiring Retirement

Run so as to win. Every athlete exercises discipline in every way. They do it to win a perishable crown, but we an imperishable one.

—1 Corinthians 9:24–25

Every day unbelievers and sinners cry, "Let us crown ourselves with roses." But our cry should be, "Let us crown ourselves with roses of the Most Holy Rosary."

—St. Louis De Montfort,
from *The Secret of the Rosary*

Alberto Salazar's life has long revolved around running, although it is only in his recent retirement from road racing that he realizes what all the miles might have meant. In his early days, Salazar often sprinted past opponents to find the answer, not unlike the young John outrunning the older Peter to reach the tomb first, only to find it empty (see John 20:4). As his career progressed, his injuries and "disqualifications" made him fear that he was running "aimlessly" (see 1 Corinthians 9:26–27), but after twelve years in persevering in running the race with "eyes fixed on Jesus" (Hebrews 12:2–3), he finally won again and realized he "did not run in vain" (Philippians 2:16). And now that the competitive road is over, Alberto is not unlike the two disciples on the way to Emmaus who encountered Jesus on the journey but could explain him fully only when their trip was complete (see Luke 24:13–35).

Alberto was born in Havana, Cuba, in 1958, the fourth of five children. While Alberto's father, Jose, was attending the University of Havana, he met another bright student named Fidel Castro, and was so intrigued by Castro's message that he briefly put pursuit of his civil engineering career on hold and became a lieutenant in Fidel's army. However, when it became clear to Jose "that Castro was turning Cuba into a Marxist state," he fled to Florida with his family in the fall of 1960. Jose then trained for the Bay of Pigs invasion (but did not see action) before finally moving his family to Manchester, Connecticut.

"When you were growing up, didn't your parents talk a lot about your family tree, how there were people of 'exceptional moral strength and talent' in the eleven generations preceding you, so your success was sort of a predestined piece of cake?"

"Actually, I thought Dad was a bit over romantic about our genealogy," Alberto told me. "I believed and still believe that God works in all of our lives." In any event, Alberto's early running interest definitely stemmed from a family member, his older brother Richard. Inspired by his elder sibling's success (Richard ran a 4:06 mile at the Naval Academy, and captained their cross-country team), Alberto ran his first timed race at nine years of age. But fate soon dealt Alberto another fortuitous hand in his quest for running success, and he was eclipsing his brother's star on the Salazar family tree.

When Alberto was about to enter high school, his dad moved the family to Wayland, Massachusetts, a town just minutes away from the midpoint of the Boston Marathon.

"Growing up, did you ever do your running along the Boston Marathon route?" I wondered.

"Sure," said Alberto. "I often ran the portion of it by Wellesley College."

"Did you imagine yourself running—and winning—the Marathon during your training?" I asked.

"I'm sure *every* kid imagines himself winning the game or event at the pinnacle of his sport," Alberto replied, "and actually running on the path where the event takes place only makes the feeling that much stronger."

Not only did Alberto train on the famed Boston course, but he began to work out with the famous Greater Boston Track Club, whose members included Dickie Mahoney, Mark Duggan, Freddie Doyle, and "the King"—Bill Rodgers. Rodgers, who at the time was already winning marathons (he would go on to win an amazing twenty in his career) in turn called Salazar "the Rookie" and taught Salazar his tactics. It worked, for in his junior and senior years, Salazar was the top-ranked high school 5,000-meter runner (by *Track and Field News*) and, upon graduation in 1976, accepted an invitation to the University of Oregon, which at the time boasted the most prestigious long-distance track program in the country. College did prove an adjustment, but it wasn't long before Salazar was back on track and "the Rookie" would challenge "the King."

After a disappointing freshman season, Salazar won the National Collegiate Athletic Association 5,000- and 10,000-meter events his sophomore season and the next year won the Collegiate Cross Country Championship as well. However, he was not yet a champion off the field.

"I read in *Sports Illustrated* that you neglected your faith for a while in college, partying and picking up women."

"That's really a bit of an exaggeration," corrected Alberto. "It's true that once you go away to college you often start enjoying your freedom a little too much, and Eugene was a sports-crazy town, one of the few places that idolized its runners. So I got a little carried away, but there were no drunken orgies or anything."

"What helped you get back to God during this time?"

"Mostly just my strong Catholic upbringing. Also joining the Fellowship of Christian Athletes helped."

"Knowing you, partying too hard was probably out of the question because running meant so much to your outlook."

"That's probably closer to the truth," admitted Alberto. "I had more problems with over-training than over-partying."

Having conquered much of the collegiate running scene, Salazar next set his sights on the pros, including "the King." Salazar's first classic duel with Rodgers came in the prestigious 1978 Falmouth Road Race. Salazar, running second to Rodgers on the 7.1-mile course, began to suffer exhaustion on that ninety-degree day but refused to quit. Crossing the finish line behind Rodgers, he collapsed, delirious, his body temperature around 108 degrees.

"Is it true you were given the last rites after that race?" I asked Salazar.

"I don't remember," said Alberto, "but I vaguely recall saying 'I don't want a doctor. I want a priest!'"

Alberto actually recovered quite quickly (after having his whole body packed in ice) and, the next year, edged out Rodgers at Freedom Hill. "I'm not going to lose," he said to Rodgers as he edged ahead to realize his first big victory over "the King."

But bouts with heat exhaustion and over-training were already catching up with Salazar. His 140-mile running weeks left him crippled with tendinitis in his left knee so excruciating that he had to quit training for the Olympics. Salazar decided to head home to Boston and write off the rest of the year . . . but God had other ideas.

"My knee injury was so bad I could barely run at all," Alberto recalled. "And I didn't want to hang around Eugene and just watch the Olympic trials—that would have been devastating. So I started to drive home, but just a few miles away [in Bend, Oregon], a car rolled into me at a stoplight, wrecking my Volkswagen. While I was waiting to have it fixed, I went on a three-mile run and, for some reason, the knee hardly hurt at all. I not only resumed training, but qualified for the Olympics. After that accident, I began to realize that God makes everything happen for a reason, because I never would have been back in Eugene [to qualify] if I wasn't in that accident."

As it turned out, the U.S. decided to boycott the 1980 Moscow Olympics, so Salazar eventually did head back East, but this time with a bit more ambition. He not only decided to enter the 1980 New York Marathon, but brashly predicted he would beat four-time defending champion Rodgers, and would do it in under 2:10—despite the fact he had never in his life run a race longer than ten miles. "Bill was the soft-spoken likable nice guy, and I was the loud-mouthed kid with the bold predictions," Salazar said of his "former" self. As it turned out, Salazar did for the marathons what Joe Namath did for the Super Bowl. By winning the 1980 marathon in a then record time of 2:09:41—also the fastest "first time" marathon ever—he set the tone for his next three seasons, a trio of years that no runner would ever have again, including Alberto himself.

While continuing his streak of medium-race milestones in 1981 (setting a five-mile record in Los Altos, and winning the two-mile in Portland and New York and the 7.1-mile Falmouth near Boston), Salazar returned to the New York Marathon that October, this time promising to break the world record. He did—shattering the thirteen-year marathon mark by over twenty seconds (finishing in 2:08:13) and blowing away his competition by running a 4:33 pace at the sixteen-mile point, a feat that is still spoken of in marathon lore.

In 1982, Salazar, despite his heavy middle-distance schedule, registered for two marathons, going for the three-peat in New York, but also running in his hometown

Boston event for the first time. Beantown was tough in the heat and, although Salazar triumphed, he was not able to shake second-place finisher Dick Beardsley until the last 100 yards of the 26.2-mile race. Following his scant two-second victory, Salazar suffered his third major race-related bout with heat exhaustion, again requiring emergency treatment. After setting American records in both the 5,000- and 10,000-meter races in Oslo in the summer of '82, Salazar then won New York for the third straight time, besting Rodolfo Gomez in a strong headwind by a scant four seconds, which was not only the closest finish ever in that event, but probably signaled the end for Salazar as well.

Back in 1982 there was no doubt that Alberto was on top in the running world, and little doubt in his mind that he could keep on winning. Alberto had entered four marathons and had won them all, was the U.S. record holder in the 5,000- and 10,000- meter, and could name several other events where his name stood as the standard to beat.

"How would you describe your faith back during those championship years?" I inquired of the now retired runner.

"I was pretty much the average Catholic. I went to Mass just about every Sunday. I had a little bit of a prayer life. I told people I had faith but in reality everything else took second place. The most important things then were my twenty-mile runs. Now on Sunday, I could almost always fit in both Mass and my runs—but if there was a conflict, the twenty-mile run would win. Intellectually I knew that God, my wife, and child were most important, but in my heart, running was my god."

And, as all false gods do in time, this one betrayed its running worshipper. The miles of training and bouts of heat exhaustion finally caught up with Salazar, and an endless series of injuries prevented him from regaining championship form. "I knew I should feel happy, that I should be thankful for everything else in my life—but I wasn't happy," Alberto ruefully recalled.

"I read that you took a trip to Medjugorje in the mid '80s. Did that help your spiritual progress?"

"Yes, it did. My dad had been urging me to go for quite some time, but finally one of the monthly messages from there spoke to my particular situation, and I took him up on it."

Of course, while the Catholic Church has not officially approved the Marian apparitions attributed to this sight, the messages are in keeping with Church teaching, and the sight of many people coming together in the sacraments is certainly inspiring.

"In a way, [worshiping] shouldn't be any different over here than over there. But [while praying at Medjugorje] all of a sudden I felt an energy, and the message, which is the same now as it was two thousand years ago, finally hit me. I felt I heard Mary speaking to me and she was asking me to change."

"Is this when you started to pray the rosary regularly?"

"I actually started that a short time before I went over there, but I continued to say it when I got back and still say it almost every day."

"Including when you run?"

"Yes. Running is a perfect time to say it. You have a quiet time non-runners don't have, a time to think. I used to daydream when I ran, but then I found you can take the edge off the hardness of the exercise by concentrating on something you care deeply about."

"Do you find the rhythm of distance running fits together well with the continuous rhythm of the rosary?" I asked Alberto, talking about a theory I expounded on in a recent series of "Running the Rosary" articles I had authored.

"I don't know if I'd go as far as you would with that, Tom," Alberto said, noting that as a competitive runner he was probably a bit too concerned with time and speed to "relax into a rhythm" during training. "Actually, when it first occurred to me to say the rosary while running I thought it might be wrong because I couldn't concentrate on the mysteries fully, but then I read some accounts of people praying while they worked, and I realized that even though they weren't praying perfectly, it was still a good idea."

"Did the sacraments also start to become more important to you at this time? For example, did the Eucharist go from being something you 'fit in' on Sunday to something you desired more than once a week, perhaps even part of your daily routine?"

"I did start to go to Mass during the week sometimes . . . but it wasn't just the Eucharist that became more important. All the sacraments did. They went from being symbolic rituals to real events that carry blessings to those who believe. But they are all important. It's just like running. Training, rest, diet, supplements . . . they're all important. You might be able to take one away for a short period of time and run okay, but over the long stretch, it will hurt you."

"You mean, for example, combining the Eucharist with the sacrament of penance?"

"Exactly. If you went to Mass all the time without ever going to confession, the Eucharist would lose its effectiveness."

"Speaking of sacraments, something important also happened during this time regarding your wife, Molly."

"Yes. Molly had always been very supportive of me and my running, being a runner herself." In fact, Molly, a former collegiate runner, holds a "record" of sorts by being the only "known" mom to not only continue to run up until the time she delivered her second child, but to still maintain a sub seven-minute-a-mile pace during her pregnancy. "Until about ten years ago, Molly was an Episcopalian, but then she decided to become a Catholic.

Molly had already shared many of the Church's beliefs, including praying to Mary to intercede for us. But when she converted to Catholicism, it certainly made the sacrament of our marriage even stronger, and we could share our lives even more completely."

So, although Alberto had become firmer in his faith, he was more flabbergasted than ever about what to do with his sport. Despite the fact he hadn't won a race in ten years, Salazar felt God was leading him to train for the 1992 Olympic marathon. After months of preparation, however, he was forced to drop out of the trials after only seven miles because of a knee injury. Afterwards, Salazar unequivocally retired—or so he thought.

"By '92 a lot of the other runners were laughing at me, and I, too, wondered if I was fooling myself by continuing to train—and after the Olympic trials, I took my injury as a sign to retire. But not long after that, I happened to run into Dr. Paul Raether. He told me he thought I was run down and if I got my hormone level back to normal [with treatments], I might be able to train competitively again.

"Did those treatments include Prozac?"

"Yes. But I want to set the record straight on that subject. Prozac was not something I took to replace spirituality. I did not take it for depression, but took it because my nervous system was so screwed up from over-training and those three serious instances of heat dehydration that my brain was no longer providing the hormones my body needed. Prozac helped accomplish this."

So after feeling good for several months and once again being able to train without pain, Alberto dreamed of a return to competition—this time the Comrades Ultramarathon.

"Why did you decide on an ultramarathon?" I pondered.

"I think it was because even though my training was going well, my speed of ten years ago never really returned, and for the Comrades [at 53.75 miles], endurance was more important than speed."

"What did people say when you entered?"

"Nike [where Alberto worked as a marketing consultant] thought I was nuts. Molly thought I was nuts. And the press thought I was crazy, because I had never run [or trained for] an ultramarathon before."

But against all advice, in May of '94, Alberto ran the South African race, a washed-up marathoner hearing the snickers of many of the other twelve thousand runners and the jeers of the hometown crowd. The first part of the race went well for Salazar, in fact, too well. By thirteen miles, Alberto was already out in front, despite his intentions to stay back in the pack. Still near the end of the first half, he felt amazingly strong physically and spiritually (Alberto had already prayed two full rosaries) and began to think he had a chance. But then disaster struck, and Alberto thought his quest had ended.

"I read that at around thirty miles you felt horrible. Were you actually walking at this point, looking for a nice grassy spot to drop out?"

"Part of the problem was my energy reserve. In a race like that, you need some kind of energy intake or your body runs out of glycogen. When I had scouted the race, I found out it was sponsored by Squeezee. Now the year before, Squeezee was handing out their carbohydrate gels every few miles of the race, and I assumed they would be doing it again—but they weren't. I had a few gel packets taped to my water bottles, but it wasn't nearly enough to get me through the race. Around this time, my supply ran out and I was running on empty.

"How close were you to stopping?"

"I was just about to sit down for good when I heard God say 'Here you are, once again, telling me you can't do it.' And I *couldn't*. Then I seemed to realize something. In the past, I could do it on my own, through my own mental toughness. But at Comrades, God finally bought me to a point where, since I physically couldn't do it, only He could make it happen." And He *did*.

"When it was over, you said that your victory was a miracle. Were you referring to the fact that you ran the last half of the race without carbohydrate intake, something you thought impossible?"

"That's part of it. No one should have been able to continue running hard for all those miles without carbohydrate supplements. But the biggest miracle was probably the change within the press corps and the crowd."

"What do you mean?"

"Well, the press was against me, still portraying me like the brash cocky kid who predicted victory . . . when all I said before the race was I thought I'd be competitive. And, of course, the crowd was against me because they wanted their countrymen to win, not an American. But when I resumed running after my brief rest, that all began to change."

"What do you attribute the change of heart to?"

"I think it was because, when I resumed running, I also started to pray the rosary again, and the crowd was not only close enough to hear the 'Hail Marys,' but they could see that I was in pain and was humbled. They could actually see a Higher Force working within me . . . and slowly but surely they all started to cheer. It was not easy, but through prayer and the fans' support, I was able to finish."

"And win for the first time in twelve years!" I added.

"That's true. Although the Comrades might not be as prestigious as Boston or New York, I now tell people it was my most memorable win. During those twelve years, although I enjoyed coaching and marketing, running was still my most readily identifiable talent, and for the first time I felt I could share my faith through victory . . . that God had validated me."

"Did you try to run competitively again after Comrades?" I wondered.

Alberto laughed. "I planned to, but a few months after that I stepped in a hole and tore some ligaments, and never regained competitive form."

"Wow. So it was all for that one race."

"Looking back, I'm sure it was a blessing," Alberto declared. "I always was an obsessive personality type, and I probably would have lost the joy that came with that win. It's like when Jesus said, 'If your eye causes you to sin, cut it out.' Some people take that figuratively, but I think God does take even good things away from people if they start to use them for the wrong purpose."

"Are you regretful in any way of all the years you lost through injuries and over-training?"

"I'm sure that if I hadn't trained so hard, I might have had a longer career. But that's also what made me win. I might have raced another ten years, but would I have run a 2:08 marathon?"

"I guess it's like saying that many of the saints would have lived longer if they hadn't fasted and disciplined themselves so much—but would they then have still been saints?"

"I don't know," said Alberto, leaving the question for the theologians to settle.

"Do your kids pray when they play sports?" I asked.

"My kids aren't runners," Alberto explained, "and although I tell them it's okay to pray before or even during their football or basketball games, I'm not sure they do. We do say the rosary together as a family, oftentimes in the car, and I really see now what a blessing they are, and how for-tunate I am to be able to share this with them—and I think they're starting to see God in me easier now that I'm retired from running and with them more."

"How's your job at Nike going? The press gives them a hard time, too."

Alberto laughed. "Tom, I was as upset as everyone else when I heard the human rights violations that were reported in our company overseas. While I didn't call up Phil Knight (Nike CEO) that next day and demand an explanation, I was concerned whether we were doing the right thing. But I think since then Nike has taken the lead and, for the most part, has remedied the problems. If I didn't think so, I wouldn't continue to work there. The working conditions have improved (for the factory workers) and while you always could pay them more, if you raised the pay to U.S. levels, the Nike factory workers would be earning more than the country's doctors and lawyers, and that would throw their economy into complete chaos, with professionals quitting their jobs to work in factories."

"I guess this is another case where there are no easy answers."

"That's true. The Nike workers do have a better standard of living than almost anyone in Vietnam, but as it is not *our* country, there is only so much we can control."

○   ○   ○

"Well, thanks again for the interview, Alberto," I said with sincere appreciation. "I'm really happy to get a fellow runner's story for the book."

"Thanks for being persistent and not giving up when your calls weren't being returned. Now that I'm retired from running, I should make time for these things. Which reminds me. I got a call from a Catholic grade school to come give a talk. When they first called, I was thinking to myself 'that school's an hour away.' But I'm not running 120 miles a week anymore, so I have no excuse not to make time to share my faith."

Hanging up the phone, I realized that ideally this is the way you'd want every story to end. Not only did Alberto Salazar finish the race well, but he now has the time and peace of mind to tell us about it.

14. Lou Holtz

The Skinny Winner Who Knows Our Souls

When Jesus saw his Mother and the disciple there whom he loved, he said to his Mother, "Woman, behold, your son." Then he said to the disciple, "Behold your mother."

—John 19:26-27

What though the odds be great or small
Old Notre Dame will win over all
While Her loyal sons are marching
onward to victory.

—from "The Notre Dame Fight Song"

Note: Before you begin reading this last profile, I want you to be forewarned. Lou Holtz is one of my favorite coaches (and Christians), so anything resembling a traditional unbiased account of this man is out of the question. Still, I invite you to hang around with us to see why I am so high on ol' Lou. I am convinced that you, too, will be filled with Holtz's hope and humor.

The first time I met Lou Holtz was in the spring of 1995 after Notre Dame had finished 6-5-1, his worst season since his inaugural campaign with the Irish in 1986, when the team he inherited from Gerry Faust went 5-6. In between those two seasons the Irish were 73-14-1, including an undefeated national championship year, a 23-game win streak, and a Heisman Trophy winner. Now in his thirty-eighth year of coaching, Holtz had previously been a college head coach at William & Mary, North Carolina State, Arkansas, and Minnesota (with a 233-107-7 record overall), but he had always maintained that Notre Dame was the place where he had most wanted to coach, and now he was living his dream. Granted, things weren't always easy for him here with the intense national scrutiny the team gets, but the chance to share his Catholic faith openly—as well as to have his own faith nourished by the school—was worth the media glare the Golden Dome created. And since I had always felt that there was a side of this Notre Dame football question that wasn't fully explored, I began this initial interview with a discussion of why people love—or hate—Notre Dame with such passion.

"Around World War I," Holtz stated, "a lot of immigration to this country occurred. Many of the immigrants were Irish and most of them were Catholic. They were the newcomers and faced a lot of prejudice finding decent homes and jobs. Meanwhile, Notre Dame was a small struggling Catholic school with a spirited sports program that most of the big universities did not want to play.

"But gradually, Notre Dame did get some games with the established programs, and not only did they [usually] win, but with the help of Knute Rockne, they won with grace and style. This gave these immigrants, the underdogs of society, hope that they could succeed also, and it was natural that many of them adopted Notre Dame as their team. Of course, their kids grew up following Notre Dame, and many of these kids ended up attending Notre Dame and experiencing the tremendous peace one feels here."

"Is that peace really our Lady's presence?" I asked.

"I don't think there's any doubt about that!" Holtz thundered, and then repeated the story about how after Notre Dame burned down in 1879, Fr. Sorin declared he would rebuild the university topped by a statue of Mary "so damn big," said Holtz, "that everyone who looks up at the Lady on the Dome will know what this place is about."

"But why then," I continued, "do other fans hate Notre Dame so much?"

"Year in and year out they're the team to beat," Holtz stated. "Notre Dame has had more All-Americans, Heisman Trophy winners, and national championships than any other school, so every school wants to measure itself against us. And, well, some Notre Dame fans *are* arrogant."

"Yes, but don't you find that most Notre Dame haters also hate God and the Church?"

"I don't know . . . there are a lot of people who hate Notre Dame football that respect Notre Dame. They like the fact that we're old fashioned—no coed dorms, no athletic dorms, athletes must maintain a higher GPA to remain eligible."

"But don't you think a lot of people who hate Notre Dame can't accept this notion that so many Notre Dame players and fans say that praying to God helps the team to play better, and, in many cases, to win?" I hypothesized.

"I don't think God cares who wins a football game," Holtz stated, before pausing just long enough to let you know something was up. "But I do think His Mother does," he added with a wink.

"Coach," I continued, "I've read that, despite your exhausting schedule, you still say the rosary every day for guidance and direction. Don't some people find it odd that a man who regularly works sixteen-hour days chooses such a time-consuming prayer?"

"Time consuming!" Holtz scoffed. "The rosary only takes me about fifteen minutes. The busier you are, the more important it is to take time to pray. If you only pray when it's convenient, you'll never find time." Again he paused. "Do you know anyone who wants to see you only when he needs something?"

"Yes," I admitted.

"After a while, you just want to avoid this person, right?"

"That's true," I confessed.

"Well, think about how God must feel about those who only pray when they need help."

"With all your commitments, Coach, are you still able to attend daily Mass?"

"During the football season I do," Lou answered, but when I began to chuckle, Holtz quickly cut in to show me this was *not* a case of religious humor. "It's not for *that* reason. During the football season, my schedule is a constant. I can go to the 6 a.m. Mass on campus, then head straight to the football office to start work. The only difference is I have to get up half an hour earlier. And what good does a half-hour of extra sleep do anyway? But in the off-season, when I'm on the road recruiting, speaking, etc., it doesn't always work out."

"How about the Grotto?" I wondered. "I know you like going there, but it's probably hard for you to pray there much during the season, because everyone recognizes you and wants to stop and talk."

"Actually, I do go there more in the summer, but that's because the winter here is too cold. And I don't like cold!" Holtz joked. "But seriously, I love to go there after business trips. It'll be one in the morning and I've just arrived home from a long flight, but I'll go to the grotto first because it will be so peaceful, so tranquil, I can put the whole day in perspective."

"Speaking about keeping things in perspective . . . Frank Leahy, during his fine tenure as head coach of the Fightin' Irish, spent so many hours preparing for football games that he often slept in his office and, during the season, went home to his family once a week or less. Now at some point, no matter how successful he was as coach, this behavior had to detract rather than add to the true Notre Dame spirit."

"You have to have the right priorities," agreed Holtz. "My first priority is my faith in God. Second is my family. Notre Dame is third. My family is far more important than my job. Now these priorities don't usually conflict, but when they do, you have to go with what's important."

"After Notre Dame, what's next on your list?" I wondered.

"My fourth priority"—and again Holtz made a dramatic pause—"is *golf!*"

"Golf?" I exclaimed.

"Yes. And fifth . . . everything else."

While Holtz has had great success coaching at four other major universities before landing the job at Notre Dame, he has found several things unique about the demands of this position. First, there are far more requests for interviews, so many that Holtz told me, "If I agreed to all of them, I would literally have time for nothing else." Second, the amount and type of mail Holtz receives is amazing. Lou gets more than a thousand letters a week, but the staggering volume itself does not tell the story. Besides the typical requests for autographs and routine rounds of advice (although one fan's suggestion that the quarterback Tony Rice throw darts to help his passing touch actually benefited the team during the 1988 championship season), there are two categories of letters that separate the mailbags of a Notre Dame head coach from those of his contemporaries. The first are those of die-hard fans seeking a friend, and the second are letters from the sick seeking a cure.

"Have you heard from Allyson Treloar lately?" I asked Holtz. Treloar was singled out in Lou's 1988 book *The Fighting Spirit* as a prime example of one of Lou's pen pals, having sent her first letter (which included a worry rock) to Lou when she was in the fourth grade and Holtz had just completed his first season with the Fightin' Irish.

"I haven't heard from Allyson Treloar in . . . " he began to grin, "almost a week." Just as I suspected! Treloar, now a senior in high school, had been writing Lou all these years. However, Holtz's last letter, sent to Allyson on her senior retreat, showed that she had come a long way from her "worry rock" days:

> *Dear Allyson,*
> *It has been brought to my attention that you are experiencing a very special weekend. I wish there were some words of wisdom I could share with you that would make this more meaningful . . . but I'm not nearly as smart as the people conducting this weekend, so my advice is to pay attention to what they say, and pray to God as He certainly answers prayers. Ask the Holy Spirit to fill you, Allyson, and I hope you will utilize this weekend to help you get through some difficult times in the future, as well as take a closer walk with the Lord.*
>
> *My best wishes,*
> *Lou Holtz*

Because of time constraints, Holtz has narrowed a once-extensive spiritual reading list to one book, the Bible. "I practically coach from the Book of Proverbs," Holtz said, only half in jest. "Read Proverbs 3:5. It will change your life," Holtz promised, so I did:

> Trust in the Lord with all your heart,
> on your own intelligence rely not.

You can certainly see this proverb echoed in Holtz's letter to Treloar or in his frequent playful self-putdowns such as "I wasn't smart enough to attend the University of Notre Dame as a student, but I'm smart enough to be the head football coach." But you really see it in Holtz's responses to the scores of letters from the sick and terminally ill, including his reply to this twelve-year-old cancer patient:

> *Dear Coach Holtz,*
> *Thanks for the hat, football and great time. I had the very best time in my life! I could not have dreamed of anything more. Thanks again!*
>
> *Dear _____ ,*
> *Thank you very much for your card. I really enjoyed having you here at the University of Notre Dame. I really wish I could have done more . . . to let you know how much we respect and admire your courage and determination . . . While I don't really have the authorization to do this, I personally want to give you an honorary position on our football team. I have never done this before, but consider yourself a member of the 1995 Fighting Irish. All you have to do is cheer hard for us and be brave.*
> *Thank you again.*
>
> *Sincerely,*
> *Lou Holtz*

"Coach, I read that when you were a kid, you were a big fan of Frank Leahy's Notre Dame teams . . . "

"Well, that wasn't hard! They went undefeated four years in a row."

"They sure did. But you also talked about how every night you went to bed and prayed to God to make you bigger, quicker, and faster so you, too, could play at Notre Dame. But when you finally realized that wasn't happening, you said to yourself, 'Why doesn't God answer prayers?' But then you realized God answered your prayer with something even better: He let you coach at Notre

Dame, where you could not only work with people on the football field but you could do it for more than one or two years. 'I've had the thrill that goes beyond compare. I've had the thrill of being at the University of Notre Dame,' you stated. But that was after the 1988 championship season, some six years [and no championships] since. Do you still feel coaching at Notre Dame is an answered prayer, a thrill beyond compare?"

"Yes, I still feel that way," Holtz confirmed. "I still love being here. As for last year, tragedy and suffering are sent to prepare you for something greater."

"A greater tragedy? Last year's record was 6-5-1. Surely there couldn't be another season more tragic than that!"

This time Holtz *did* laugh. "I do think God is preparing me for something greater, but that's not necessarily confined to football."

After briefly touching upon the subject of retirement, my first heady meeting with Holtz had ended and, while I was quite impressed by his steadfast faith, I couldn't help but ponder what his prophetic talk about tragedy and suffering meant. Surely, I thought, his words were fulfilled when, early in the 1996 season, a spinal condition sent Lou to the Mayo Clinic for emergency surgery. But Lou bounced back after missing only one game—and so did the Irish, who upon Holtz's return won their last six regular season contests to finish 9-3. At the time, I thought his predicted suffering had ended. Little did I realize that the tragedy had just begun.

Holtz's next season at Notre Dame would also be his last. The 1997 season still had a couple of more contests left when Holtz resigned the only job he ever wanted, and had loved above every other. Although the Irish were enjoying another fine season, they had already lost two games and thus had been eliminated from a chance for the national championship. "This will give the university time to find a new coach before the recruiting season begins," Holtz stated. "And I've prayed over this decision, so I know it is the right one."

The reasons for Holtz's departure from beneath the shadow of his beloved "Lady on the Dome," as he often called the university's patroness, will perhaps never be fully known. Holtz has consistently refused to address that question, giving me but a partial answer when he said, "Tom, I will never go into all the reasons I left—but you are right in saying I did not want to break Rockne's record" (for most wins at Notre Dame, something Holtz would have done with just one more season, as Rockne finished 105-12-5 and Holtz 100-30-2). Holtz did seem to feel some distress over the fact that, for whatever reason, a new athletic administration began denying Holtz athletes who were only average students in high school but whom he considered possessing a strong enough character and work ethic (i.e. Chris Zorich, Tony Rice, etc.) to make it academically at ND. Ironically, Randy Moss, the current all-pro wide receiver for the Minnesota Vikings and the last Holtz recruit to be denied admission was later kicked out of the notoriously lax Florida State program—but Holtz still feels he could have straightened Moss out. And of course, Holtz was not particularly overjoyed with being offered only a one-year contract in 1996 after his first two contracts were for five-year terms, years that included one national championship and two #2 finishes.

Still, some of this is more understandable in the light of history. When a new university president took over in the last four years of Frank Leahy's tenure, he cut football scholarships drastically and Frank, feeling he could no longer maintain his own lofty standards (87-11-9 with four national championships but none in his last four seasons) also resigned after finishing his last season with a record of 9-0-1! And many historians felt that the university would have eased out even Knute Rockne in a couple of more seasons had he not died in that fateful March plane crash, for many priests felt his football coaching figure was beginning to overshadow other aspects of the university. Indeed, Rockne often drove the Irish administrators crazy. He not only constantly entertained outside coaching offers, but actually signed a contract to coach at Columbia when the Holy Cross Fathers decided Notre Dame could no longer play in bowl games—only to change his mind later and finagle out of that ill-fated decision with a little legal help.

But perhaps in many ways, Holtz's decision to depart Notre Dame in 1997 goes back to 1993. In the second-to-the-last game of the season, Notre Dame had beaten Florida State 31-24, and only Boston College stood between them and Holtz's second undefeated regular season. However, to the shock of just about everyone in Notre Dame stadium that afternoon, Notre Dame found themselves trailing the Eagles 38-17, with only eleven minutes left. But inspired by their never-say-die coach, the Irish, led by the senior QB Kevin McDougal, scored 22 straight points and staged what appeared to be one of the greatest comebacks in Irish history, taking a 39-38 lead with just over a minute to play. However, aided by what an official later admitted was an incorrect roughing penalty on the kickoff, Boston College started in good field position and, after ND defensive end Pete Bercich missed what appeared to be a sure interception, quarterback Glenn Foley drove the Eagles into field goal position and David Gordon kicked a field goal as time expired, which allowed Boston College to pull off the upset.

As hard as that roller coaster game was for Holtz to take, what transpired after the bowl games was even more disheartening. Notre Dame and Florida State (both finishing with only loss) each defeated tough bowl opponents that New Year's Day. Based on the fact that in 1989, when the Irish and the Miami Hurricanes both finished with one loss, but Miami beat Notre Dame in head-to-head competition and thus was voted #1, Holtz figured that it was now Notre Dame's turn. Instead, the football writers voted the national championship to Florida State (or more correctly, to their popular coach Bobby Bowden), and Holtz feared that he had just lost a "beauty contest," that his lack of appeal with the media cost his team the title. Lou felt his fears were confirmed when the story came back to him that when Notre Dame had lost a game, a sizeable amount of the press box—many who had a vote in the championship poll—had cheered. "Those journalists were supposed to be impartial," Holtz said. "I thought their bias toward Notre Dame cost us the votes we needed." Holtz admitted that the sportswriters' attitudes bothered him; he even hinted that if his own lack of popularity among the voting press was keeping Notre Dame from glory, perhaps he should step aside.

Again, Holtz is right on most accounts. In former days, journalists were supposed to be unbiased, but sportswriters have long been exempt from or have ignored that tradition, and are generally the most cynical of a notoriously hard-hearted lot. Notre Dame, with its positive moral teachings, will always have more foes than fans among the media. Furthermore, Holtz, who has always built up his competition and downplayed his own team's chances before games—to the point he was nicknamed "Boo-Hoo Lou" by his media buddies—knows many of them would vote against his team if there was even the slightest justification.

But know that Holtz's Notre Dame dilemma is nothing new—and perhaps not even all that bad. Forty years before Holtz, the media also chided Leahy for unrealistically decrying his great team's odds against lowly opponents, but Frank still won national championships by not losing any games and thus not giving writers any choice. True, once in a while a great coach will come to Notre Dame and, perhaps by not completely buying into the Catholic part of the Notre Dame tradition, will sometimes get the benefit of the doubt from the press. This was true for Holtz's friend Ara Parseghian, when he coached Notre Dame to a controversial 10-10 tie with Michigan State but Notre Dame still was voted the championship over the unbeaten Spartans. Generally, Notre Dame has to meet higher standards in everything they do to get the same accolades as secular schools, and football is no exception. If, like Parseghian, Holtz had garnered two national championships instead of one, history no doubt would have considered him, along with Ara and Rockne and Leahy, as one of Notre Dame's (and college football's) legendary coaches. And yet, none of these great coaches can surpass Holtz in the amount of spiritual impact he has had on lives, including the effect the following letter had on a struggling young Catholic author. Written days before his Notre Dame resignation, when there were certainly far more important things for him to do, Lou wrote:

> *Dear Tom,*
> *Thank you very much for your letter. I really*
> *appreciated the article you sent. It is easy to see*
> *why you are successful, Tom, because you pay*
> *great attention to detail and let absolutely noth-*
> *ing slip by you. I consider you a true friend.*
>
> *Sincerely,*
> *Lou Holtz*

More than two years had passed before I caught up with Holtz again in the autumn of 1998. Holtz was out of coaching (for the first time since attending college as a student) and was on a book tour promoting his motivational bestseller entitled *Winning Every Day (The Game Plan for Success)*.

"The book is dedicated to the women in my life," Holtz said without prompting, realizing from past conversations that I was likely to veer off on subjects beside the book. "My daughters, Luanne and Liz, my mother, Anne, my mother-in-law, Eleanor, and the finest person I have ever known, my wife. Beth . . . "

"How's Beth doin'?" I asked.

"She's making good progress in her throat cancer treatments," Lou told me. "A doctor originally misdiagnosed her throat condition and the cancer went undetected for six months. She is the most courageous person I've ever known . . . And last but not least, I dedicated the book to our blessed Lady on the Dome."

"I wanted to ask you about our Lady, Lou. When we last talked, you said you didn't think God cared about who won a football game, but that our Mother did. Now I know that Notre Dame response was at least somewhat in jest—but doesn't God care at least somewhat about the game itself?"

"God cares about everyone. He really truly cares about each and every one of us. And since He cares about all of our hopes and dreams, in that way God cares about the game, if not directly with the outcome."

"But I know what you mean about our Lady," I told Lou. "Coach Davie [Bob Davie, current head coach of Notre Dame], who is Presbyterian, had a hard time identifying her place in these things when we talked. So I told him to think about her as Notre Dame's biggest fan. Just as the fans at Notre Dame stadium don't actually participate in the game but somehow help the Irish to win, Mary's 'divine cheering' must have something to do with Notre Dame's success."

"I think the analogy of Mary as #1 fan is correct. As I've said before, I think she has a lot to do with Notre Dame's never-say-die attitude."

Pleased with his approval, I moved on to another controversial issue. "Coach, in his book *The 100 Yard Lie*, writer Rick Telander of the *Chicago Sun-Times* makes an eloquent point that because football players have become so much bigger, faster, and stronger in the last twenty years, there is now too much potential for serious, permanent injury and the game has become too violent for a civilized society. Now that you've stepped away from coaching, what are your thoughts on the subject?"

"No, I would not classify football as a violent sport," Holtz asserted. "It is a sport that requires physical toughness, and a game in which a team must be physical to execute properly; but played properly, it is not supposed to be violent."

Feeling confident, I threw in my own theory on this subject as well. "Actually, Coach, I think football may be the modern version of the 'just war.' Augustine talked about a just war in terms of a clear moral objective, no unnecessary violence, no killing of civilians, etc., and while modern weaponry seems to preclude this type of war, football satisfies all the criteria, as a team can obtain and defend territory, not to mention uphold morality, in a physical but fair fashion. Do you agree?"

"I think there's a lot of truth to that," Holtz replied. "After World War I, football became very popular in this country, and I think a lot of people thought of it as their team going to battle. You could almost say back then that men traded one set of helmets for another."

To have Lou Holtz accept two of my faith and sports theories in one day was almost too good to be true, but I continued. "Coach, I know Mike Ditka, although he has recently tried his darndest to control it, has had trouble harnessing his emotions and has been know to swear at players [and fans] on occasion. Has that ever been a problem for you, coaching in this emotional sport?"

"When I was younger, I did swear on rare occasions," Holtz admitted, "but I immediately felt bad about it. The only word of that nature I did use when I was older was 'ass'—and that is found right in the Bible." Here, Holtz paused. "But I'm not proud of that either."

"One thing I'm sure you are proud of is your regular participation in the Mass."

"Yes, the Mass has always been important to me. It started when I was an altar boy, and now it sets a spiritual tempo for the day."

"Can you explain why the Mass is so important?" I asked.

"I'm sure there are better qualified people than me to do that," Holtz said humbly. "Or you can look in the Bible or the [Catholic] *Catechism* to find an explanation. I'm not . . . "

"Perhaps, for the kids who read this book, you could talk a little bit about why you go."

Holtz, seeing duty now, took a deep breath and began. "Well, when you are young, you generally are going to have your doubts, and wonder if the Bible is really true. But as you get older, you start to see the historical authenticity of the Bible, and you realize that Christ did die on the cross for us, and that he did resurrect and appear to the apostles. And I think then you also realize that Jesus really did turn the bread and wine into his body and blood, and the Holy Spirit helps generate the faith in us to see that it is the same transfiguration that takes place on the altar at Mass, and it is Jesus' body and blood that we still receive at Mass today."

In some ways, I would have liked to have stopped there and ended the story with Holtz's declaration of faith, but duty urged me to press on.

"Coach, in your book *The Fighting Spirit* [and retold in *Winning Every Day*], you tell the story of the unsuccessful salesman who was unmotivated at his job until he noticed a gold automobile he wanted. He sat in the car, then put a picture of it on the bathroom mirror and in other strategic spots around the house, and suddenly began to sell like crazy. One year later, he went to the dealer, pulled out the full amount in cash, and drove the car home—only to find his wife had now placed a picture of a diamond ring on the mirror."

Holtz laughed. "Yes, I use that story a lot."

"But what exactly is the moral message of the story? It seems like the man and his wife are driven by purely materialistic goals without any spiritual motive."

Holtz did not answer immediately, but seemed hurt when he did.

"Morality is not my purpose in telling the story," Holtz replied. "The purpose is motivation. I am not a member of the clergy . . . every story I tell does not have a moral. If it helps motivate someone, fine; if not, they are free to turn elsewhere. But a *good* salesman does care about his clients . . . " I felt it was a fair question as a Catholic journalist, but as a friend . . . perhaps it was the wrong thing to ask. For here was a definite conflict, the conflict between monetary and spiritual goals that Holtz (or few of us) hadn't quite yet solved. But with Holtz, the key word is always *yet*.

But if Holtz struggled with this question, the same could be said about his favorite university. "Coach, did you ever have trouble maintaining a Catholic identity for the Fighting Irish, as many of the players weren't Catholic?"

"No," was the decisive answer. "The players who weren't Catholic still had to attend the pre-game Masses, and still said the prayers with us before we went out of the tunnel. While there was no attempt to convert them, they knew that Catholicism was an important part of the team identity."

"How about the university as a whole?" I asked. "Do you see Notre Dame's Catholic identity slipping?"

"I haven't seen that. When I came to Notre Dame approximately eighty-five percent of the student body was Catholic, and I believe the percentage is still the same."

"But what about the faculty? As Notre Dame brings in more and more non-Catholic teachers, not to mention taking in more and more donations from non-Catholic sources, don't you think there is potential danger in Notre Dame becoming a secular university?"

"I don't know . . . I'm not sure what the faculty percentage is."

"Well, see if you agree with this statement. This is from an article I wrote for a Catholic magazine, some of which was edited out because the tone was too strong . . . one second, let me find it . . . okay, here we go. *'Besides the threat of commercial corruption from without, anyone who has read the works of Notre Dame's Fr. McBrien and several non-Catholic professors knows that there is a real threat to Catholicism from within as well. But unlike Harvard or Yale, Northwestern or Southern Cal, all former Christian universities that are now secular schools, Notre Dame has the weapon to combat all heresies; namely Notre Dame herself. The modernists may have their day, but like the song says, Notre Dame will win over all. For the modern infidels to take control here, they would have to blow our Dame off the Dome, rip the heart [the Eucharist] out of Sacred Heart [Church] and lastly, rock by rock, tear the Grotto apart. And legions of her sons and daughters would willingly die martyrs before they would allow that to happen.'"*

"I agree totally!" proclaimed Holtz, as fired up as I. "The Notre Dame faithful would die for their school before any of those things would happen."

◆ ◆ ◆

"So how is Lou?" asked Allyson Treloar, still Holtz's number-one fan after all these years. After failing in her attempt to get into Notre Dame (my letter of recommendation did not do the trick), Treloar was accepted at St. Mary's across the street and was now finishing her final year of studies. Treloar has since landed a job at Eastside Catholic High School near Spokane, Washington, teaching and coaching—something Holtz would surely be proud of.

"Hanging in there, Allyson. As you know, South Carolina did not do well at all this year, and he's had a lot of family illnesses and tragedies to deal with lately."

"That's too bad. Maybe I should write him . . . I haven't written him since he left."

"He would like that," I told her. "Now, in your relationship with Lou, which has stretched from the fourth grade through college, what would you say is the most important thing you've taken from it?"

"He impressed upon me how important a part faith plays in your life," she said. "Part of it was the fact that whenever I wrote a letter to him, he would always write one back. That really impressed me, because he was the head football coach of the greatest team in the country, while I was just a kid."

"What advice did he give you in his letters?" I asked.

"There were two things Lou mentioned quite often," Allyson said. "One was the Golden Rule—to 'do unto others as you would have them do unto you.' The second was that when you do something, don't just 'do it,' but do it *right*."

"Kind of a spiritual version of Nike," I said as Allyson laughed. "But didn't your parents say those same things, too?"

"Sure they did," Allyson said. "But hearing them from Lou somehow made it easier to believe—and follow."

"In other words, they were a positive reinforcement from someone you looked up to."

"Definitely. And you can never get enough of that when you're growing up."

"No, you can't," I told Treloar, although after talking to Lou again, I realized that sometimes you need reinforcement when growing older, too.

○   ○   ○

"Tom, I can't talk long today. I can give you only a few minutes. But don't worry. I talk fast!"

Yes, it was Holtz on the line, fresh from his first season as head coach of the South Carolina Gamecocks, a team for which he had served as assistant over thirty years ago.

"I'll try to be quick, Coach," I said. "Are you still able to go to Mass every day, Coach?"

"There is one at 8:30 a.m.—but I rarely can go as generally we are in the middle of coaches' meetings by then. At Notre Dame, I could go because the 6 a.m. Mass preceded my coaching responsibilities."

"Do you still say the rosary and read the Bible every day?"

"Yes, I do."

"Any specific Bible verses that stood out this year?"

"I can't think of any right now, but I still read the Bible every day for inspiration and guidance. And it has certainly helped me though this past year."

"I'll bet! Speaking of last year, a verse from Job might be appropriate. Not only did your team go 0-11, in September your son [and offensive coordinator] Skip, was in the hospital with chest pains, in October your wife had her adrenal gland and a non-cancerous growth removed, in November your mother died, and in December, Dewey 'Sonny' Foster went down in a plane crash shortly after piloting you to see a recruit. I know it's difficult, but do you have any comments on last fall's events?"

"Skip is okay now, but he was really hurting and I should have made him go to the hospital earlier. Beth was very serious; I wouldn't have gone back into coaching if I knew all that would happen with her, but her courage has brought her through and she's recovering again. My mom was eighty-two, and while it was certainly a sad day, she had always hoped her children would bury her instead of the other way around. And Sonny—he had become a good friend and it's still hard to understand. He was coming back to pick me up when it happened . . . I could have easily been on that plane then . . . "

"You have always been able to make friends everywhere you coached, and you stated in *Winning Every Day* that we should 'demonstrate compassion for everyone, especially those who seem callous or spiteful.' But later you go on to say that because of your busy work schedules, you haven't always done so and that, 'I don't regret any effort I've made on behalf of others but I do regret those times I missed a chance to make a difference in someone's life.'"

"Yes, from time to time, because I was so preoccupied with football, I did miss those opportunities. I think as you grow older, you begin to realize what's really important and strive to not miss those chances."

"Speaking of callous or spiteful people . . . a lot of writers will look at your 0-11 record last season and then laugh at the fact you just authored a book called *Winning Every Day*. How do you answer your critics, to show them that despite last season's record, you are still a winner?"

Holtz had clearly been preoccupied with something during the interview, but the last question, with what had already transpired, proved to be more than he could deal with.

"I don't give a damn about what the critics say! The only people I have to please are God and my family. And right now, I'm awaiting word to see if my thirty-one-year-old pregnant daughter has ovarian cancer and . . . I wish you good luck with your book, but that's all I have to say!"

❖   ❖   ❖

For several days after that conversation, I wondered—wondered not only if Lou's daughter was okay, but about the whole Holtz story. Why did Holtz have to leave the job he loved, and why, when he finally did return to coaching, did he have to become subject to so much suffering on and off the field. But then, when I read in the paper that now Fr. John Smyth was asked to leave the job he loved at Maryville for another position in the Chicago archdiocese, I began thinking this all was crazy . . . until it finally struck me.

The answer to all my questions were found in one word: *obedience*. God, sometimes directly and sometimes not, asks us to leave positions we think are perfect in order to remove any imperfections we might still have, imperfections that keep us from Him. If Smyth's obedience to his religious superior after all these years as "the man" at Maryville is his final step toward sainthood, perhaps Holtz had to leave Notre Dame and endure so much suffering in order to learn to put spiritual goals ahead of material ones. Like Leahy, he realized after leaving Notre Dame that without coaching, "There was no real sense of purpose to my life." But unlike his predecessor, Holtz *did* go back into coaching, his vocation.

Then, after enduring his worst season ever, Holtz faced two starling realities that were to influence his future choices. First, he saw his friend's life end in a crash that easily could have ended his own. Then on December 12 (the Feast of Our Lady of Guadalupe), he saw his wife (who this time was given only a ten-percent chance of surviving her latest bout with cancer) make what doctors called a miraculous recovery. Beth—as well as the other "Lady"—had always been the one who had urged him on in coaching, who, even after Notre Dame, had told him to get back into it. With these experiences of life and death,

Holtz knew he must continue. Only this time, after suffering so many losses, he would not only be able to teach people how to win, but how to win *again*.

Postscript

After finishing 0-11 last season, Lou Holtz's 2000 South Carolina Gamecocks stunned the college football world by storming out of the gates with a 7-1 start before finishing the season with 8 wins, including an improbable 24-7 thrashing of Ohio State in the Outback Bowl on New Year's Day. This not only brought Holtz the Southeastern Conference Coach of the Year Award (Lou finished second in the Associated Press C of Y voting), but it kept alive his unparalleled achievement of bringing each losing college program he inherited to a bowl game within two years.

Most observers felt Holtz was back when not only did his Gamecocks stun ninth-ranked Georgia 21-10 in the second week of the season, but the classic Holtz humor returned after the game when he declared, "I'm not going to say we were lucky to beat Georgia, but I *am* glad it isn't two out of three." But the followers of Holtz's spiritual side began to believe again with the statement he made at mid-season.

"If you look at the religious atmosphere of this Carolina team, it has changed tremendously (since last season)," Holtz stated. "About ninety percent of the players were in the chapel the other day . . . their self-confidence, their love for each other is remarkable. It's almost like a miracle. I can't account for it."

But someone can. It is *the* Fan, *His* Fan . . . our Lady.

And the miracle is that now, simply because two or more have gathered in his name, Mary's presence is just as powerful in South Carolina as it is in South Bend.

Photo Credits

John Smith: Sports Information Office, University of Notre Dame

Lenny Wilkens: Otto Greule, Allsports Photography, Inc., New York

"Rudy" Ruettiger: Rudy International, Henderson, NV

Suzie McConnell-Serio: Doug Pensinger, Allsports Photography, Inc., New York

Bobby Allison: From the personal files of Fr. Dale Grubba

Danny Abramowicz: Michael C. Hebert, courtesy of the New Orleans' Saints

Mike Ditka: Vincent Laforest, Allsports Photography, Inc., New York

Cammi Granato: Scott Levy, Bruce Bennett Studios

Ray Meyer: © J. Przepiorka

Sammy Sosa: Brian Bahr, Allsports Photography, Inc., New York

Dave Wannstedt: Courtesy Miami Dolphins, Davie, FL

Tara Lipinski: Olive Brunckill, Allsports Photography, Inc., New York

Alberto Salazar: Alvin Chung, Allsports Photography, Inc., New York

Lou Holtz: Jeanette O'Toole